LONDON: THROUGH A LENS

CONTENTS:

Editor's Note:

Welcome to 'London: Through a Lens', a beautiful photobook collection of London's most iconic sights.

Each image in the book has been carefully selected to capture a monument or an area of the city in just one frame. All photos are accompanied by a short summary of the sight presented. Photographers are credited on each page directly.

This book does not aim to be a complete collection of every sight or area in London. Instead, it focuses on some of the most well-known views of the city as they appear in 2018, as well as some lesser known spots. In a city that is continuously evolving, it is easy to take for granted that the London we see today may not be the same city before us tomorrow.

Enjoy,

G. Costa
- Also the author of 'Amazing London Walks' and 'The Independent Guide to London' (both available now)

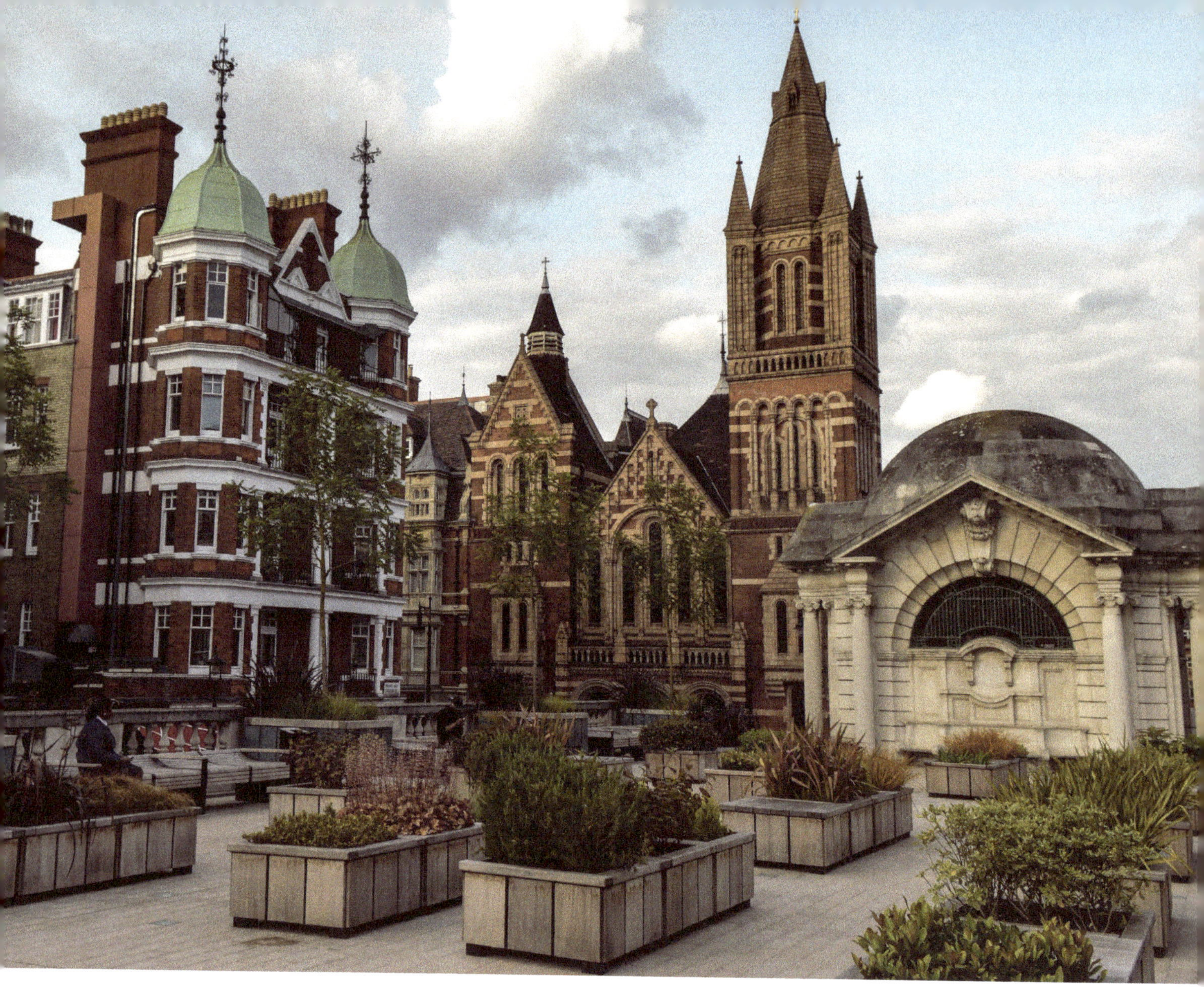

Mayfair

Photo by Francisco Anzola

Mayfair is one of London's finest and most prestigious areas. The area's name derives from the May Fair which took place here in the first two weeks of May in the 17th century. The land here was developed by the Grosvenor family in the 17th and 18th centuries. Pictured above is Brown Hart Gardens which is built on top of an electricity substation.

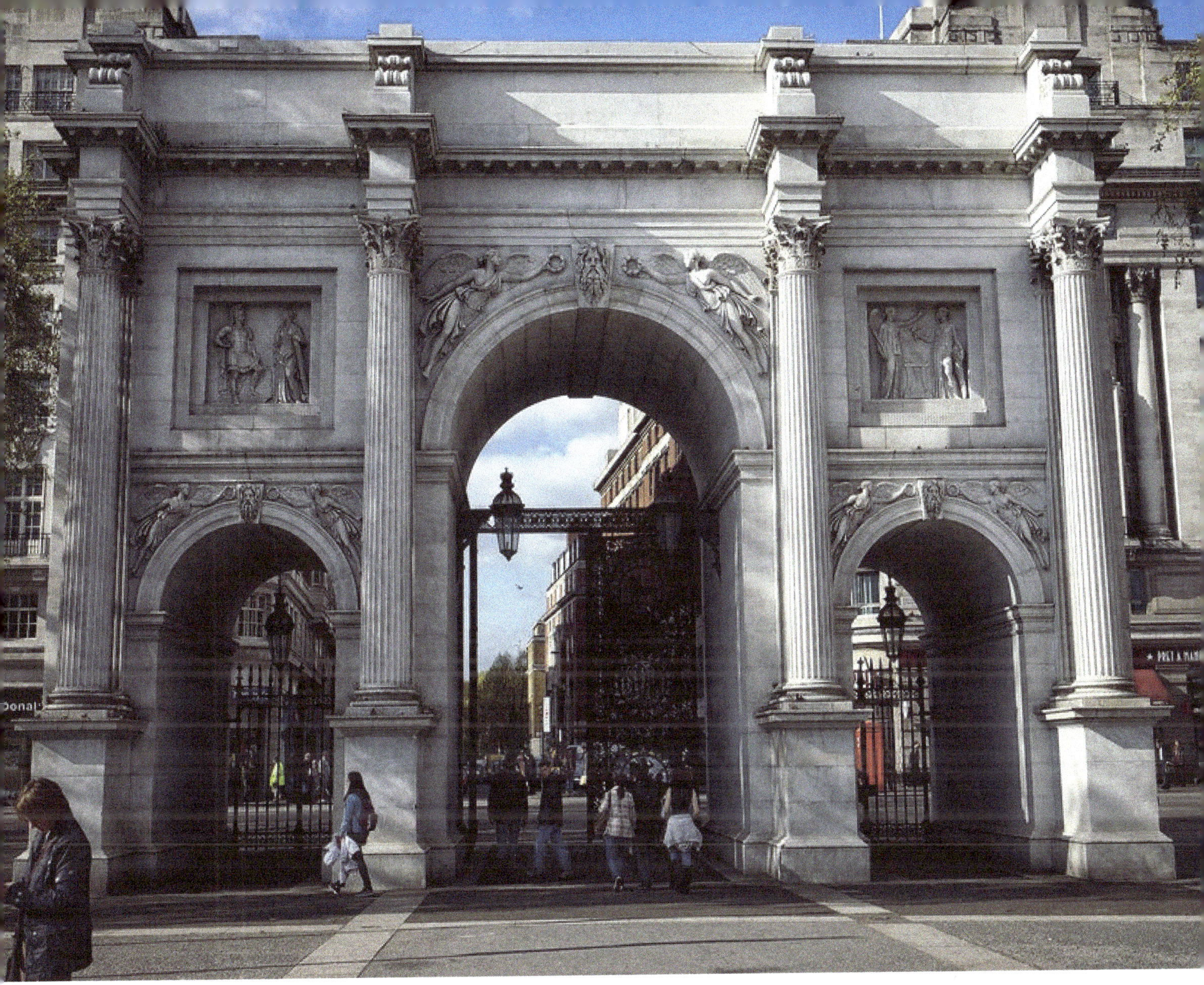

Photo by Paul Hudson

Marble Arch

Located at the western end of Oxford Street, this area was previously known as Tyburn and was a notorious spot for public executions. The marble arch standing at the centre of the roundabout today was designed by John Nash in 1827 as the state entrance to Buckingham Palace; it was moved to its current location in 1851 to aid the palace's expansion.

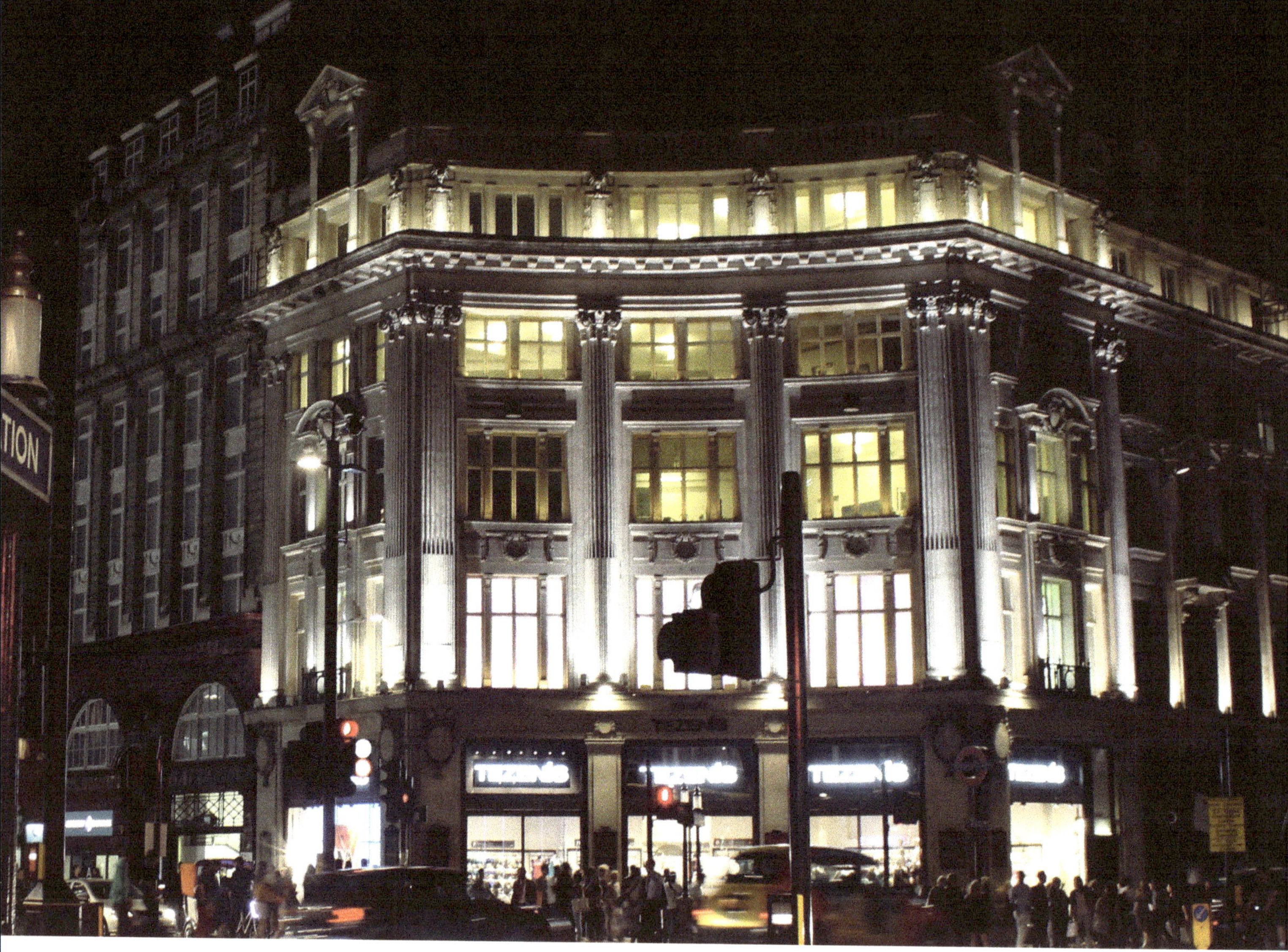

Oxford Circus

Photo by Pavlina Jane

Oxford Circus is a major intersection where two of London's busiest shopping streets intersect: Regent Street and Oxford Circus. The "circus" in this location's name derives from the Latin word for "circle" - all four corners of the crossing have buildings which curve inwards so as to create a circle when viewed from the air.

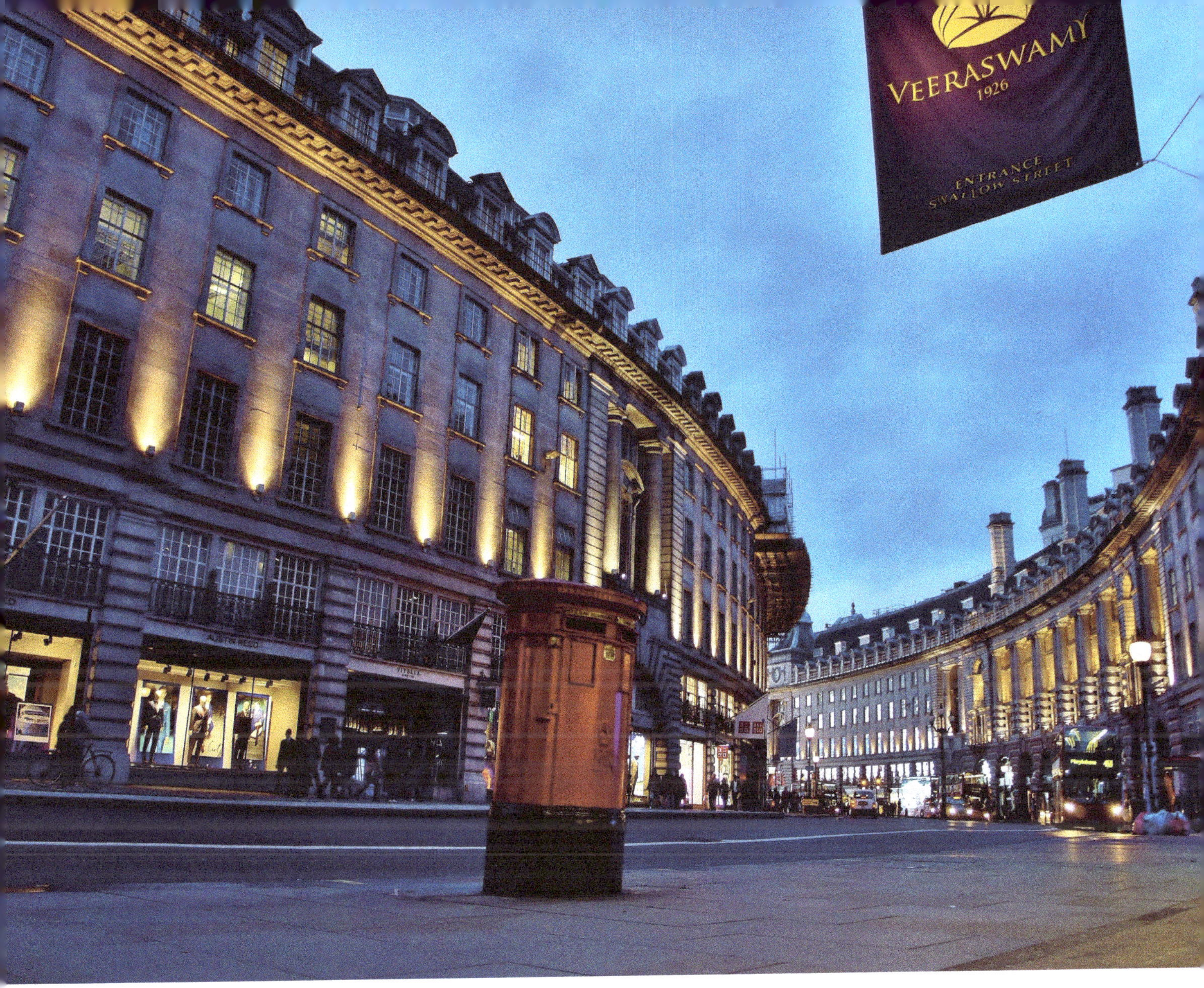

Photo by Manish Prabhune

Regent Street

Regent Street is a major part of Regency London - the part of London which was master-planned and built in the early 19th century. The street was designed by John Nash (who also designed Marble Arch) and was modernised in the 1920s. The majority of the street is owned and operated by The Queen's Crown Estate.

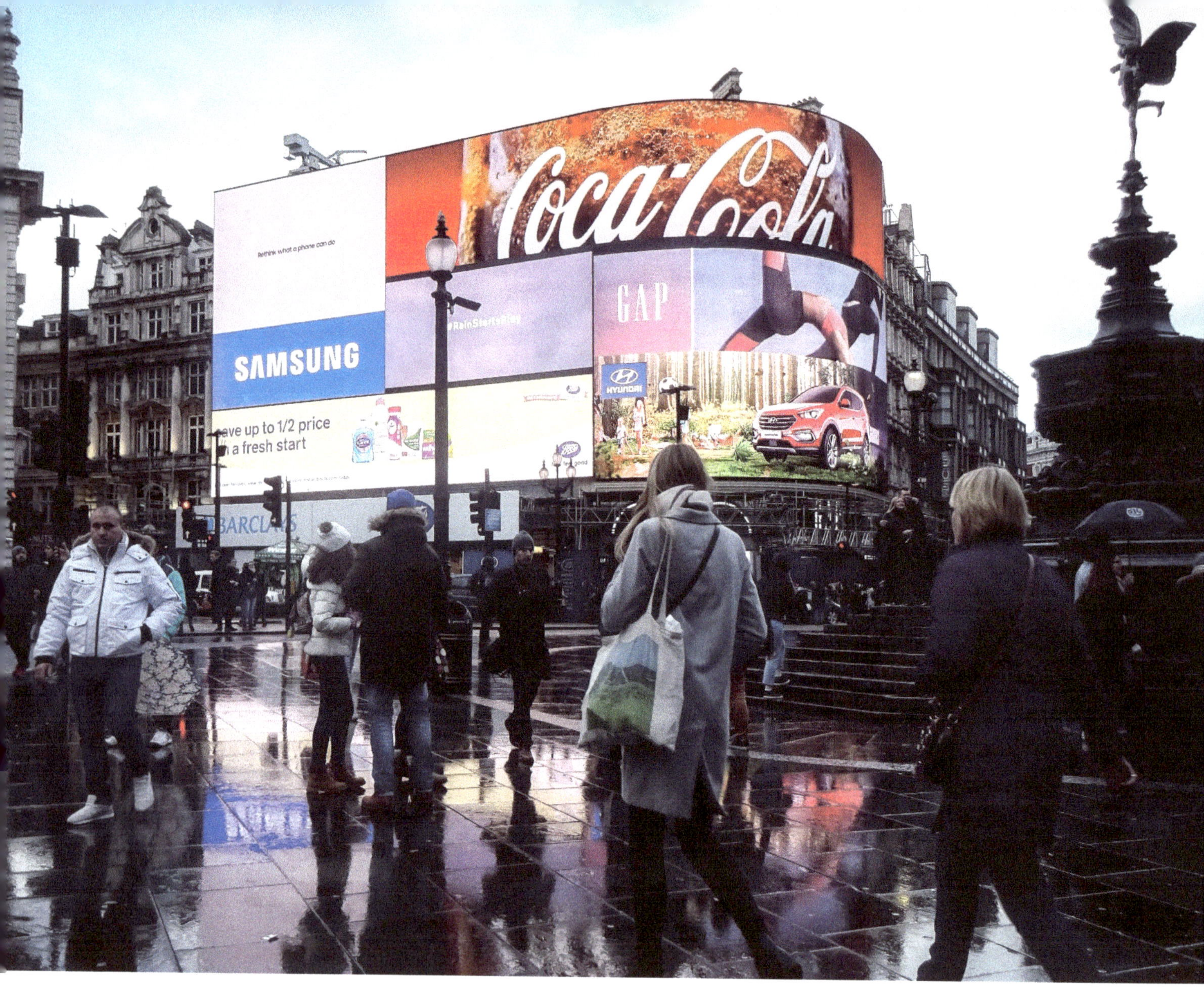

Piccadilly Circus

Photo by Garry Knight

Piccadilly Circus is located in the heart of The West End, London's immensely popular theatre and nightlife district. This major intersection has featured electric advertising signs since 1908, with Coca Cola having advertised here continuously since 1954. To the right of the photograph is the Shaftesbury Memorial Fountain dating from 1893.

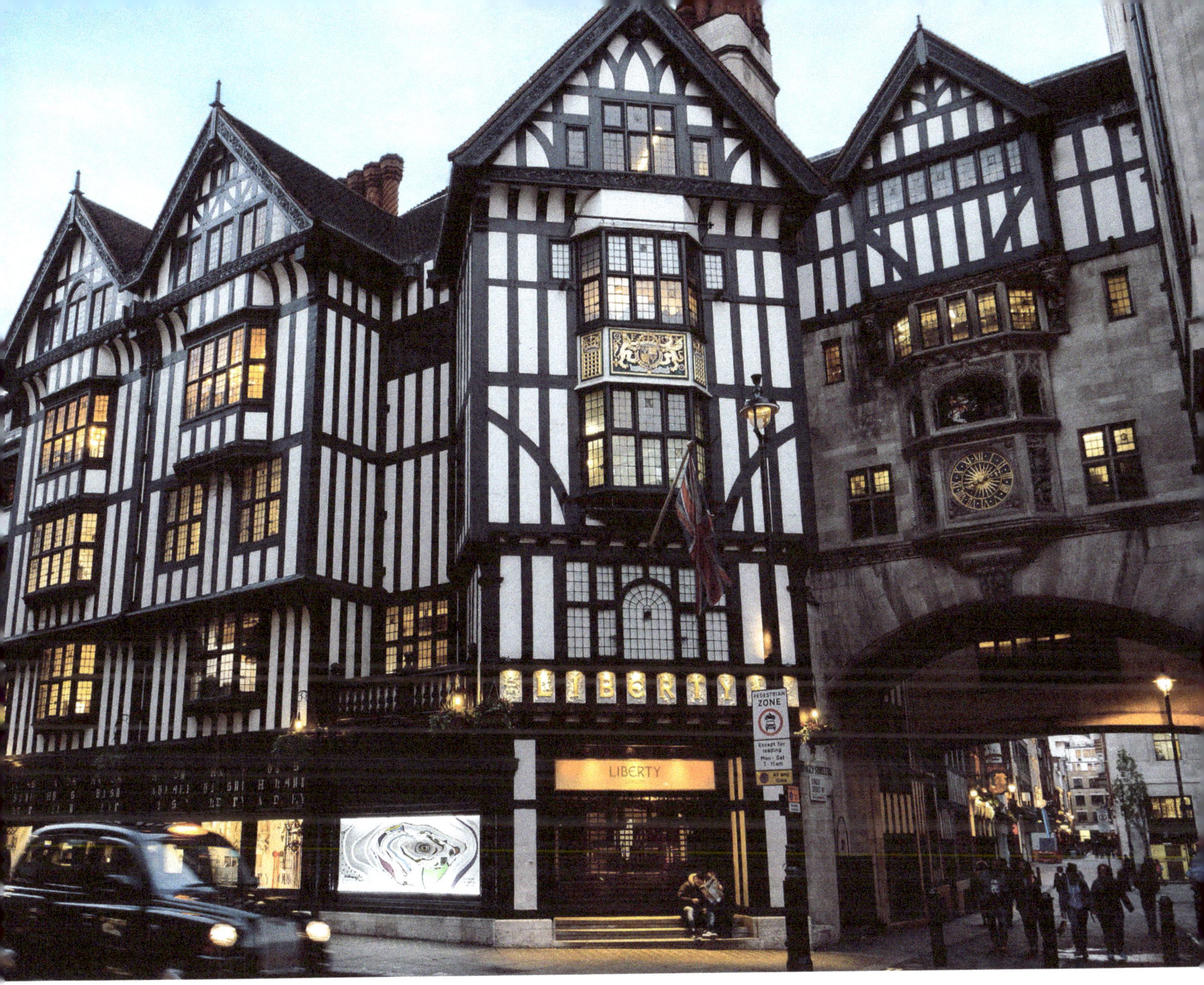

Photo by Stig Nygaard

Liberty

Liberty's mock Tudor facade is difficult to miss. This luxury department store on Great Marlborough Street has stood on this site since the 1920s, although the company was founded a few decades earlier in 1875. Liberty is particularly well-known for its scarves, rugs and floral patterns, as well as the colourful prints used across its range of fabrics.

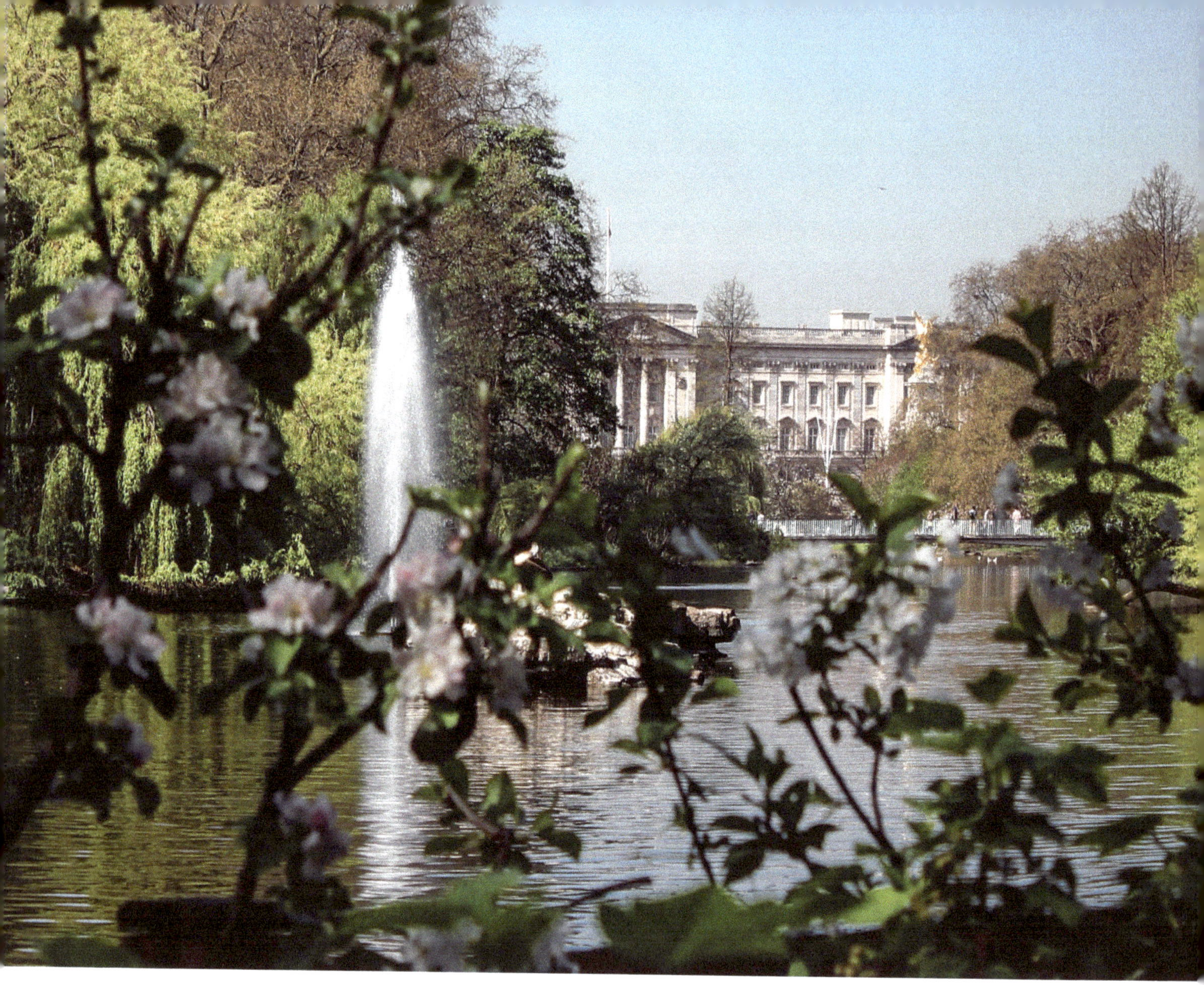

St James's Park

Photo by Katarina Dzurekova

St James's Park was originally part of York Palace owned by Cardinal Wolsey, which was seized by King Henry VIII in 1532 and renamed Whitehall Palace. In the early 17th century, James I ordered the gardens be re-landscaped and these gardens soon became home to exotic animals. Charles II redesigned the park once again and opened it to the public.

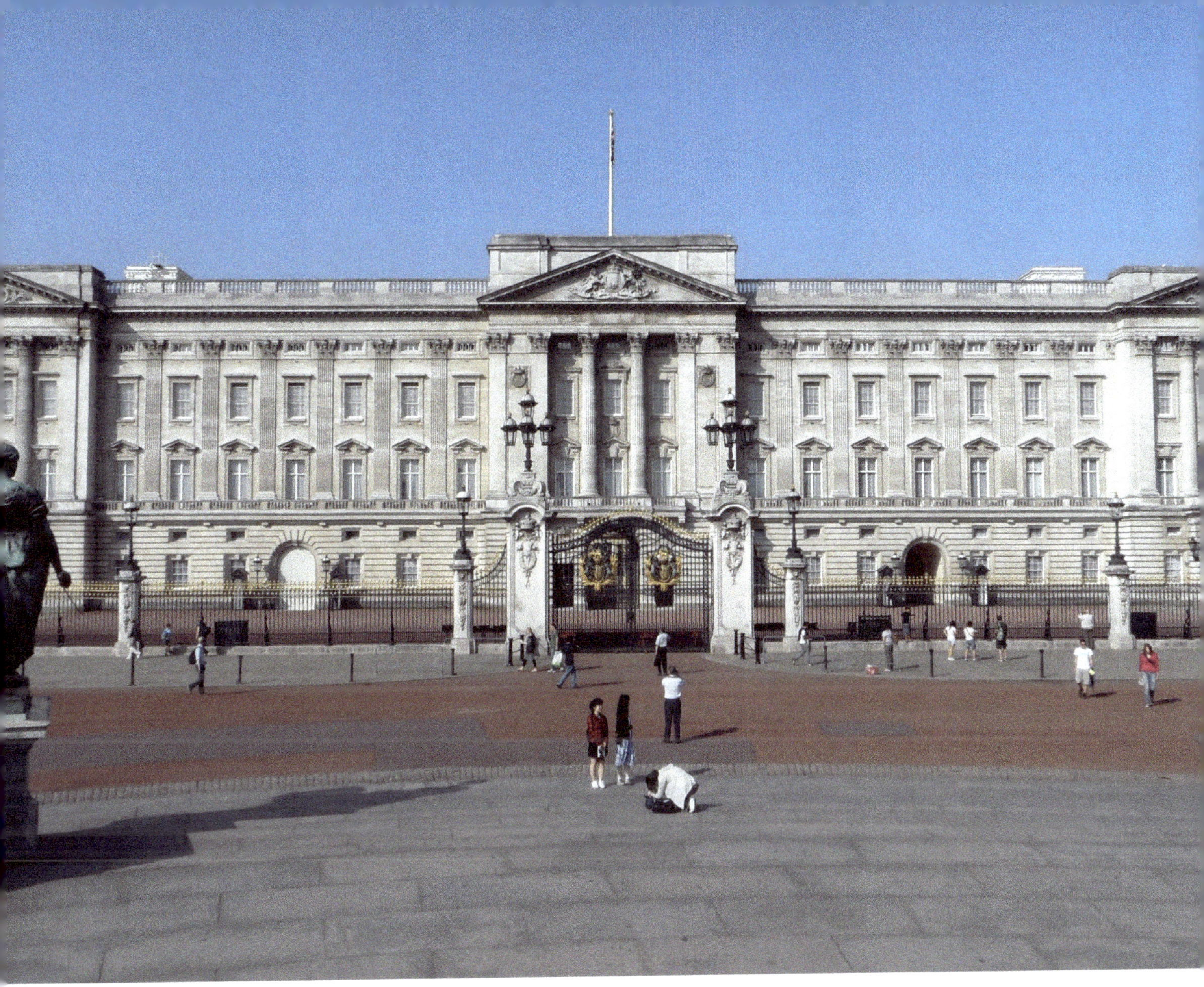

Photo by Shelley Rodrigo

Buckingham Palace

Originally home to the Duke of Buckingham, Buckingham House (as it was known then) was acquired by King George III in 1761. The first monarch to use it as their official London residence was Queen Victoria in 1837. Today it boasts 775 rooms, including 19 state rooms and 78 bathrooms. The palace has its own post office, cinema and doctor's surgery.

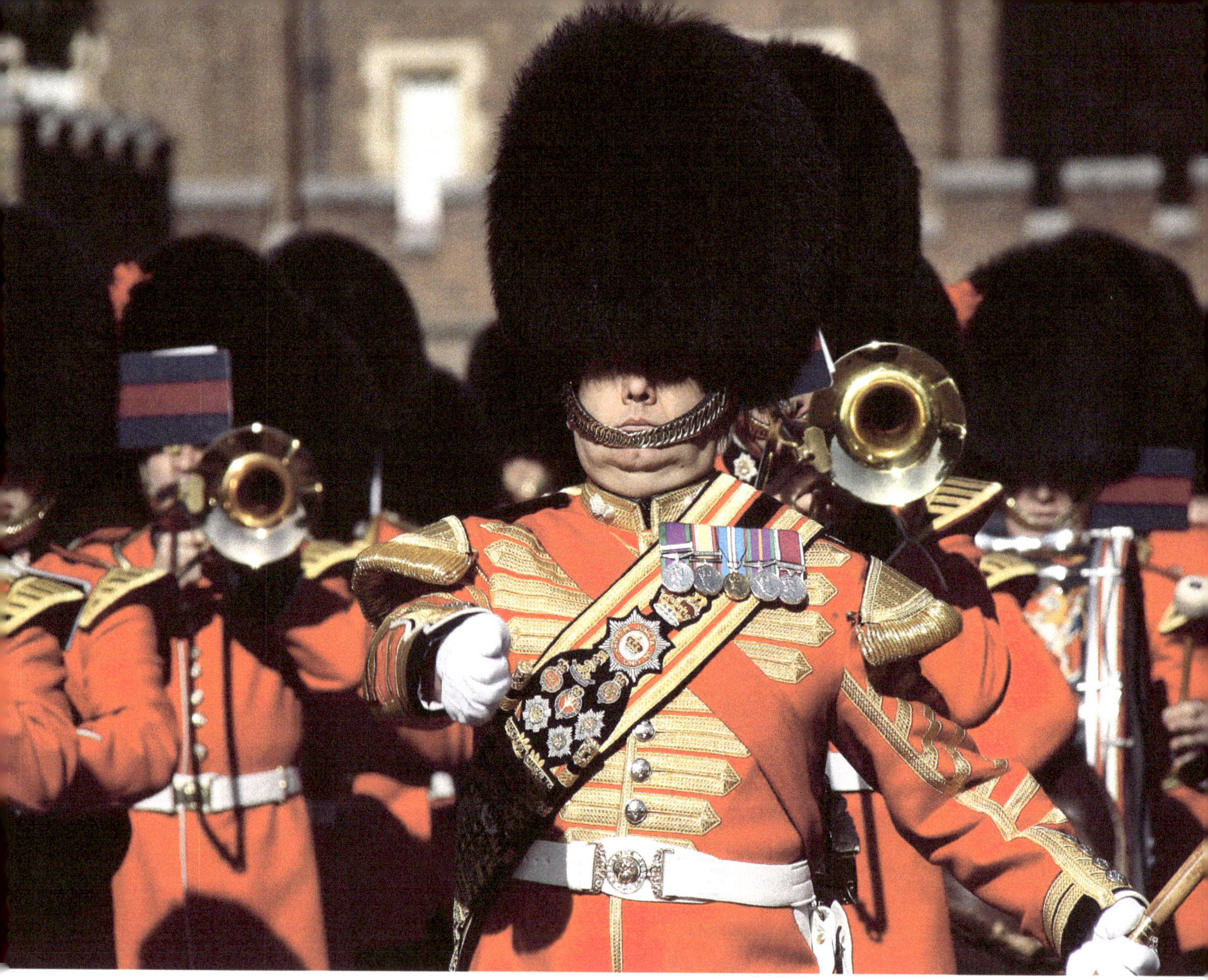

Changing the Guard

Photo by Allan Henderson

The Queen's Guards can be seen outside royal residences such as Buckingham Palace, Windsor Castle and St James's Palace, as well as at the Tower of London. These soldiers have one of the most famous shift changes anywhere in the world, with a marching band. The ceremony takes place daily in summer and four times per week in other months.

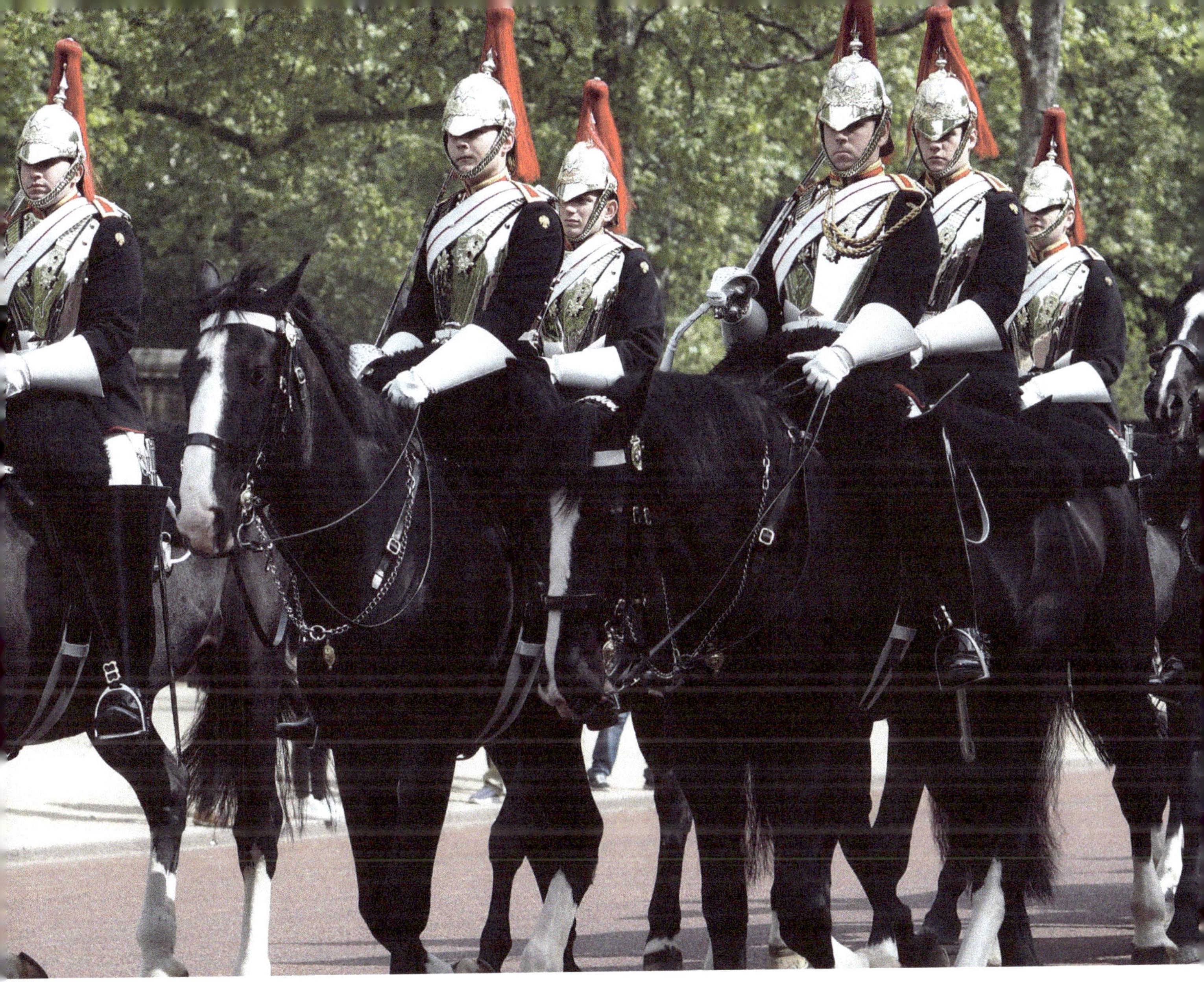

Changing The Queen's Life Guard

Photo by 'Ungry Young Man'

You will find the Household Cavalry guarding the entrance to Horse Guards Parade on Whitehall, where they have been standing guard since 1660 upon the Restoration of King Charles II. Every day at 11:00am (10:00am on Sundays), you can see the two regiments (The Queen's Life Guards and The Blues and Royals) swap at Horse Guards Parade.

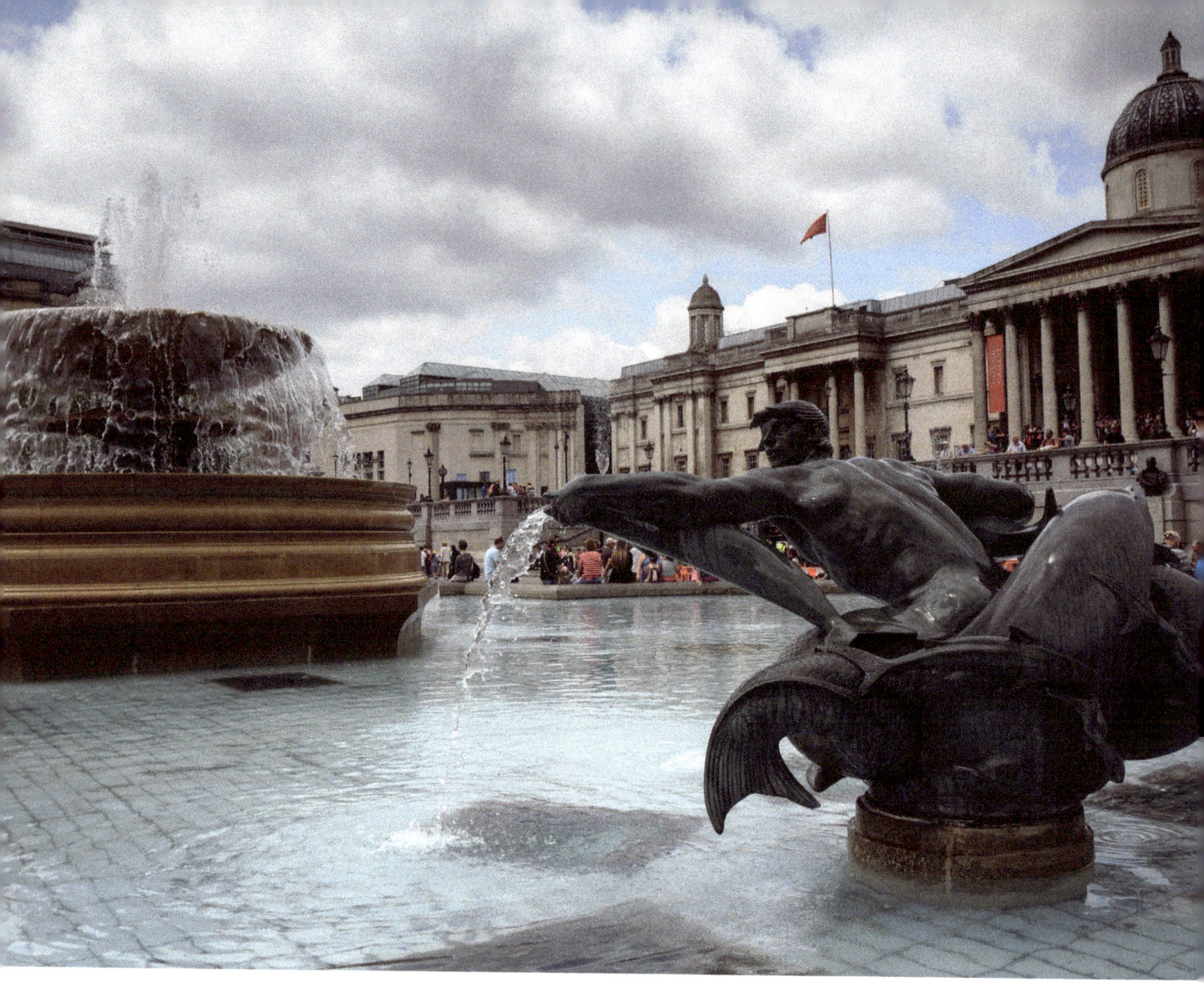

Trafalgar Square

Photo by Gary J Wood

Trafalgar Square remembers the Battle of Trafalgar in 1805 in which the British Royal Navy took on the French and Spanish Navies. Despite being outnumbered 33 ships to 27, Admiral Lord Nelson led the British to victory. The square was laid out in the 1830s by John Nash and features the imposing National Gallery designed by Charles Barry.

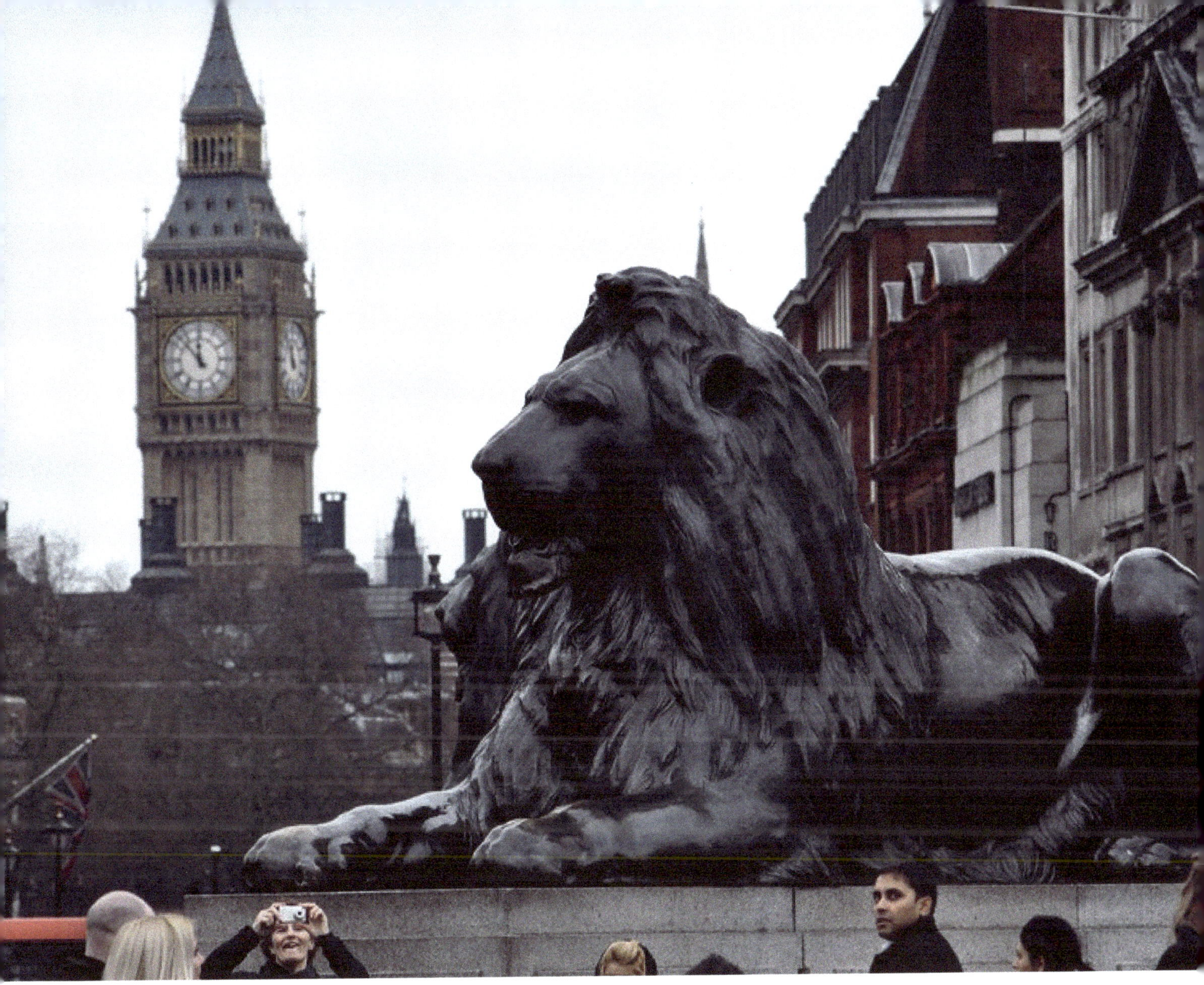

Photo by Jon Sears

Trafalgar Square

The southern portion of Trafalgar Square features Nelson's Column commemorating the famous admiral, surrounded by four bronze lions sculpted by Sir Edwin Landseer; the bronze is said to come from cannons seized from the French and Spanish fleets. Whitehall, a major thoroughfare, connects Trafalgar Square to Parliament Square and Big Ben.

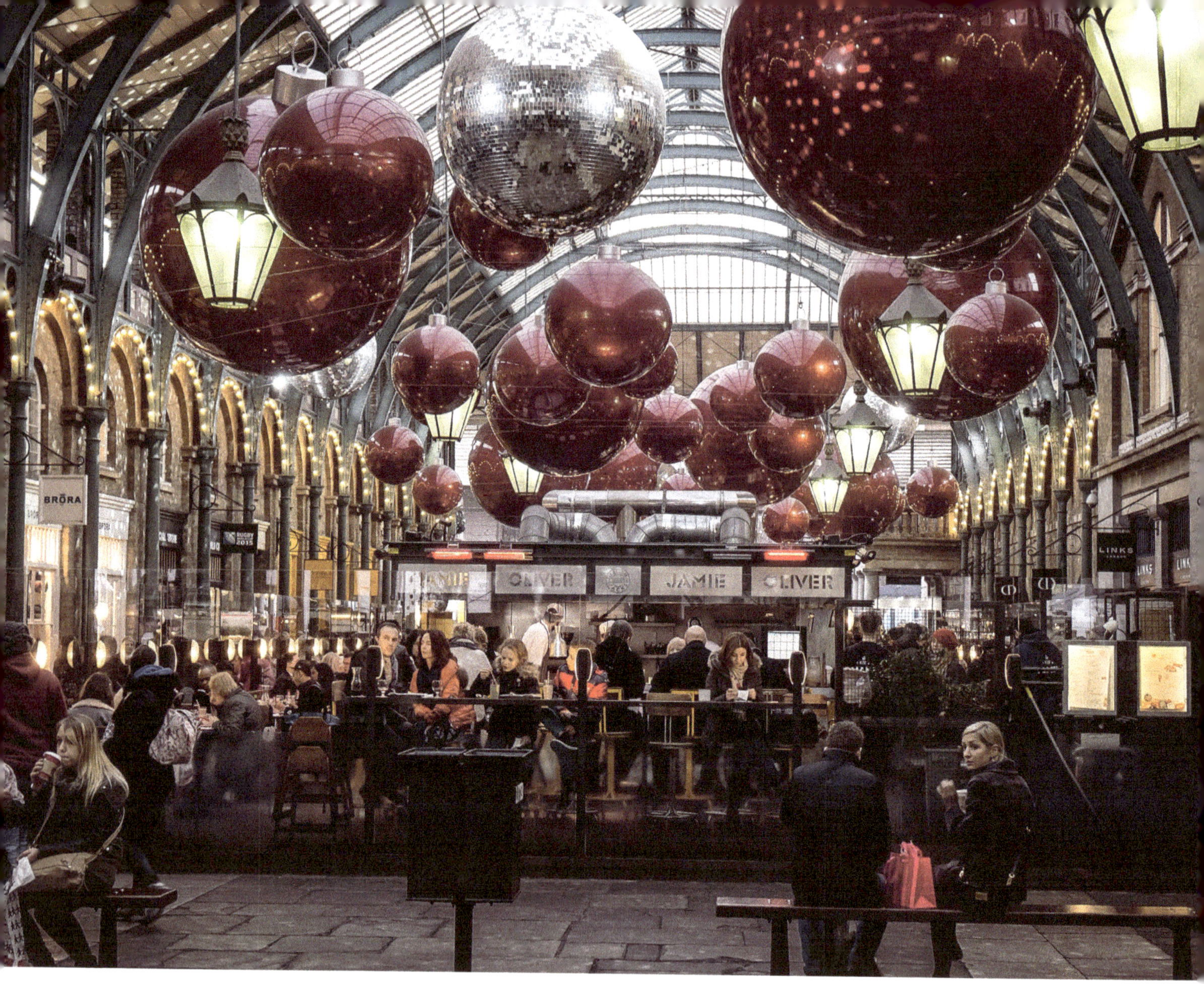

Covent Garden

Photo by Garry Knight

Covent Garden was originally part of Westminster Abbey's land. It was seized by King Henry VIII after the Dissolution of the Monasteries in 1540. It then became part of the Bedford Estate and was a fashionable and affluent area in the 17th century, but by the 18th century Covent Garden had become a notorious red-light district.

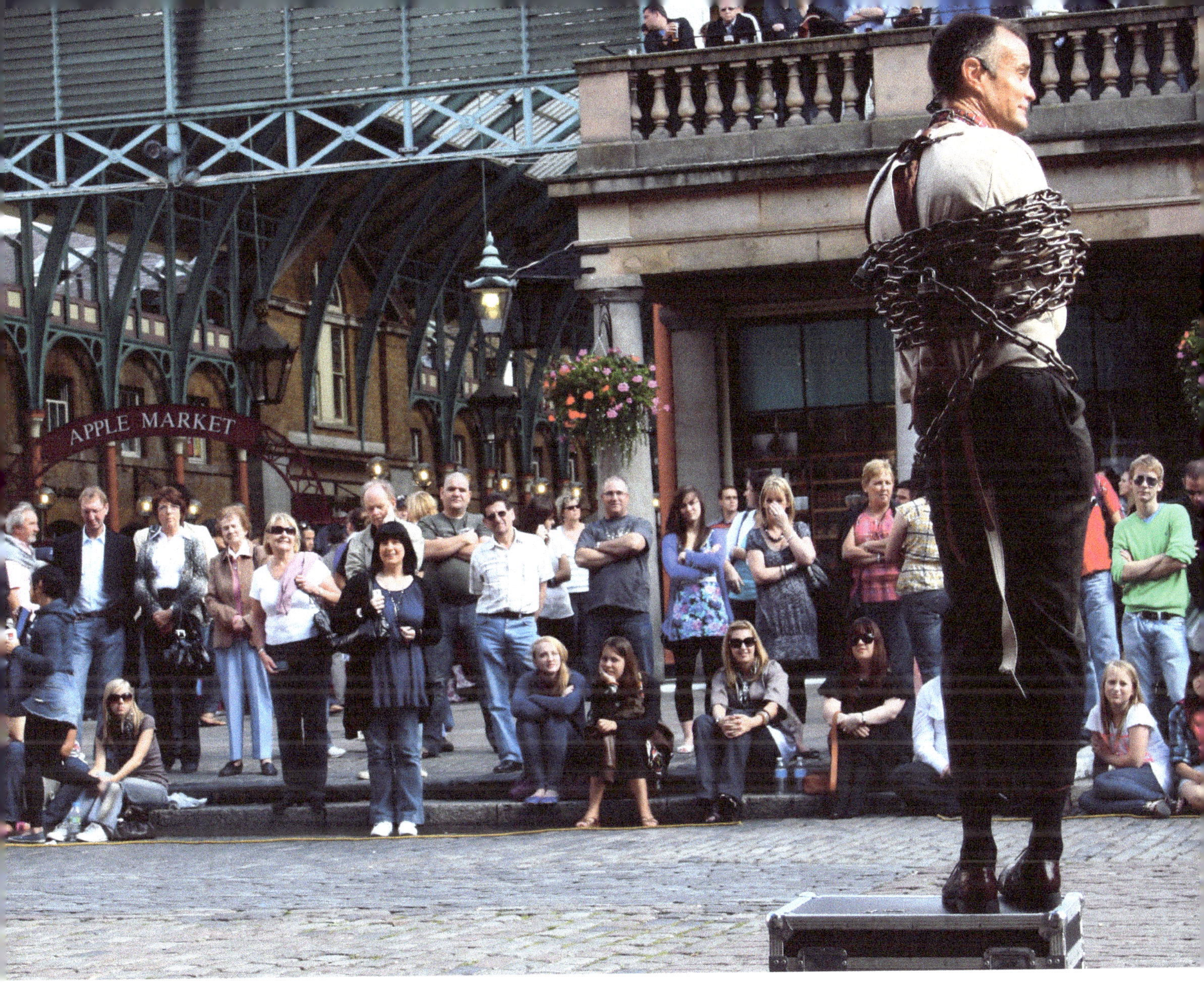

Photo by Anthony Kelly

Covent Garden

Covent Garden has been a fruit and vegetable market since the 1650s, and this continued until the 1970s. Today Covent Garden's main market building has been converted into a shopping centre. Street performers (such as the one pictured) can be found around the main piazza, from musicians to escapologists and jugglers to mimes.

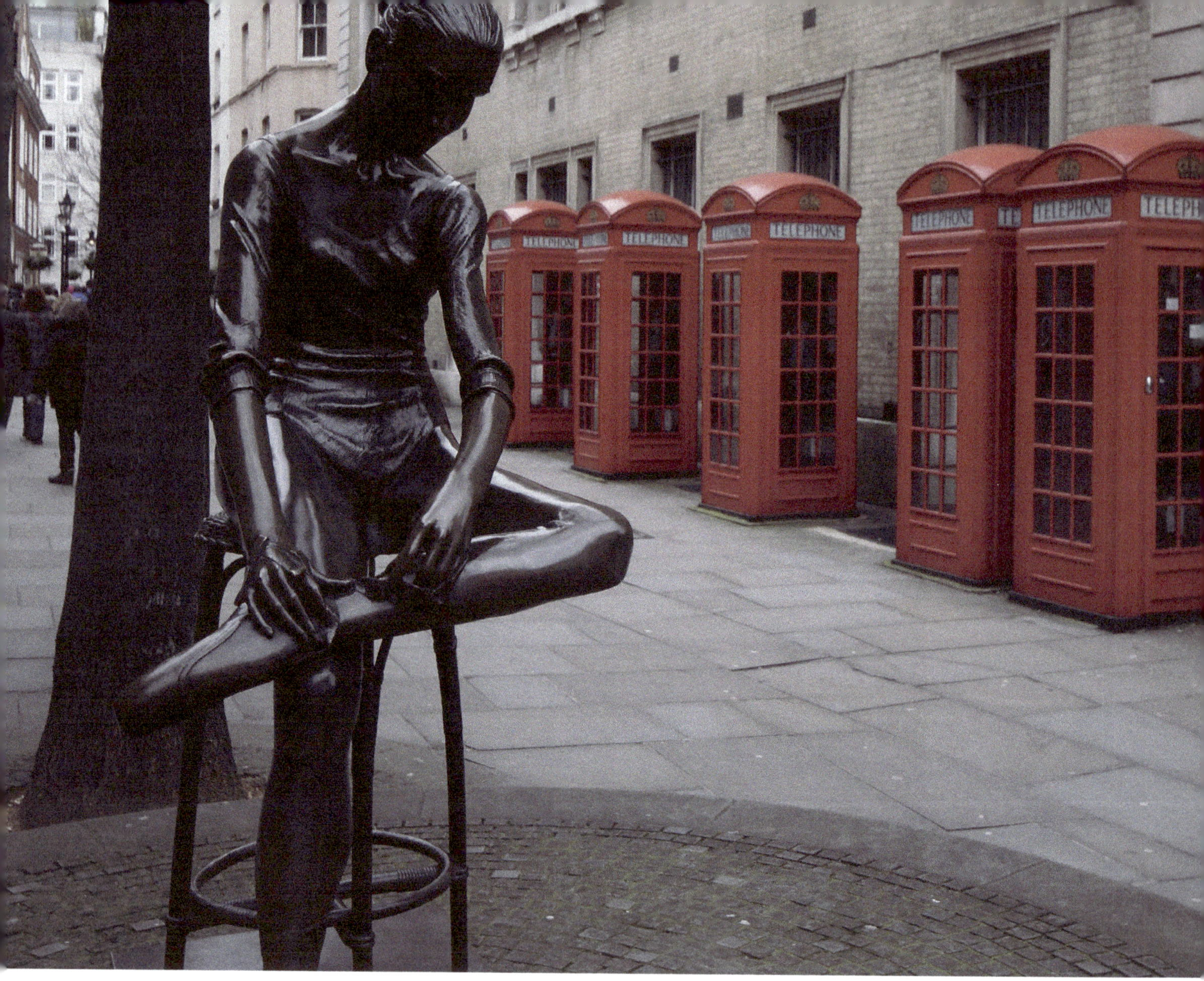

Covent Garden

Photo by Martin Pettitt

Covent Garden is also today home to the Royal Opera House, St Paul's Church, the London Transport Museum, as well as countless theatres and restaurants. The sculpture pictured is "Young Dancer" by Enzo Plazzotta and can be found on Broad Court, opposite the Royal Opera House which has been home to the Royal Ballet since 1946.

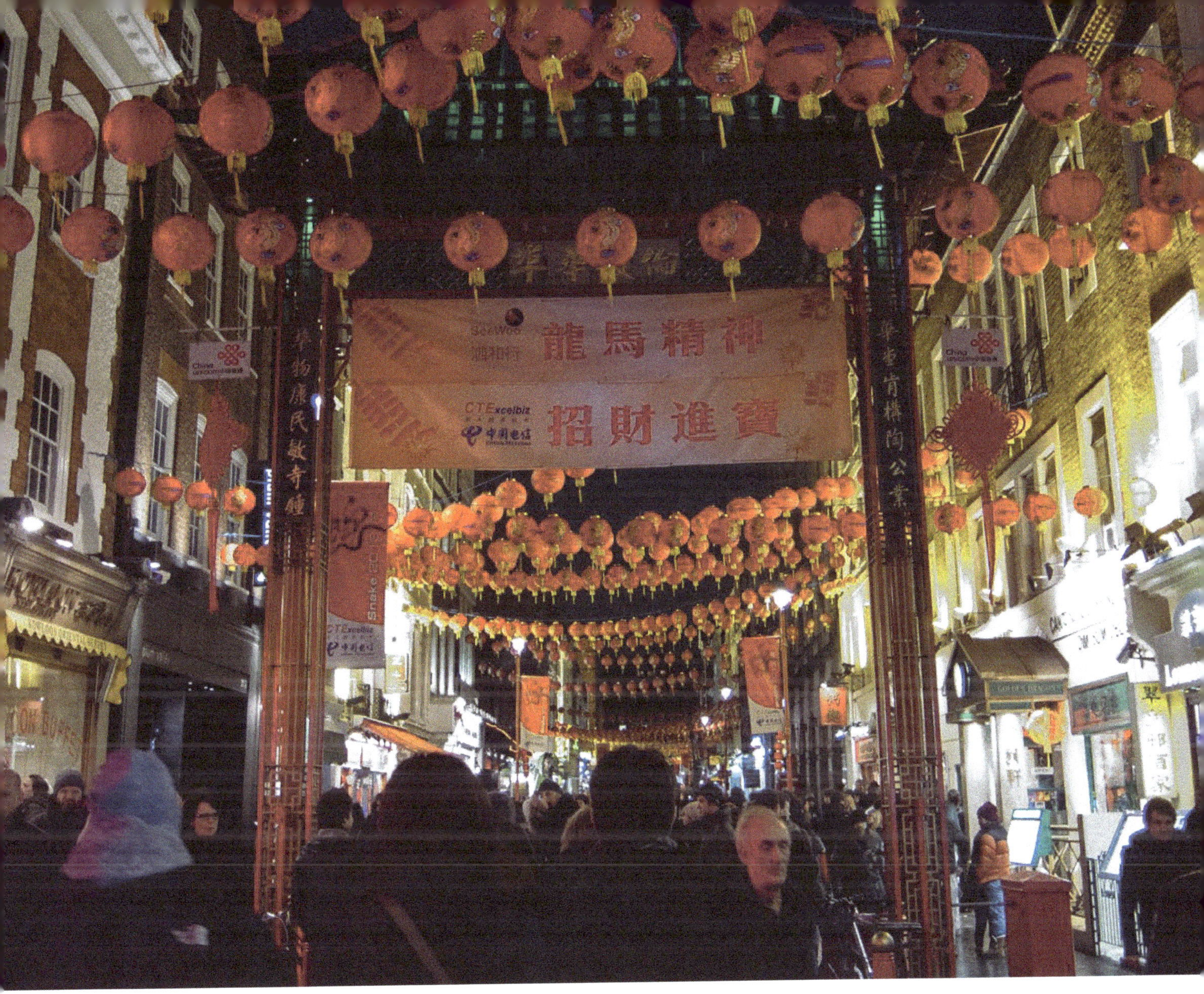

Photo by Leo Wan

Chinatown

Based in the heart of London's West End, Chinatown is a recent addition to the area having only appeared on the scene in the 1970s. Previously, Chinatown was based in London's East End, but after the area suffered heavy bombing during The Blitz and asian food increased in popularity, Chinatown relocated to its prime position in the city's West End.

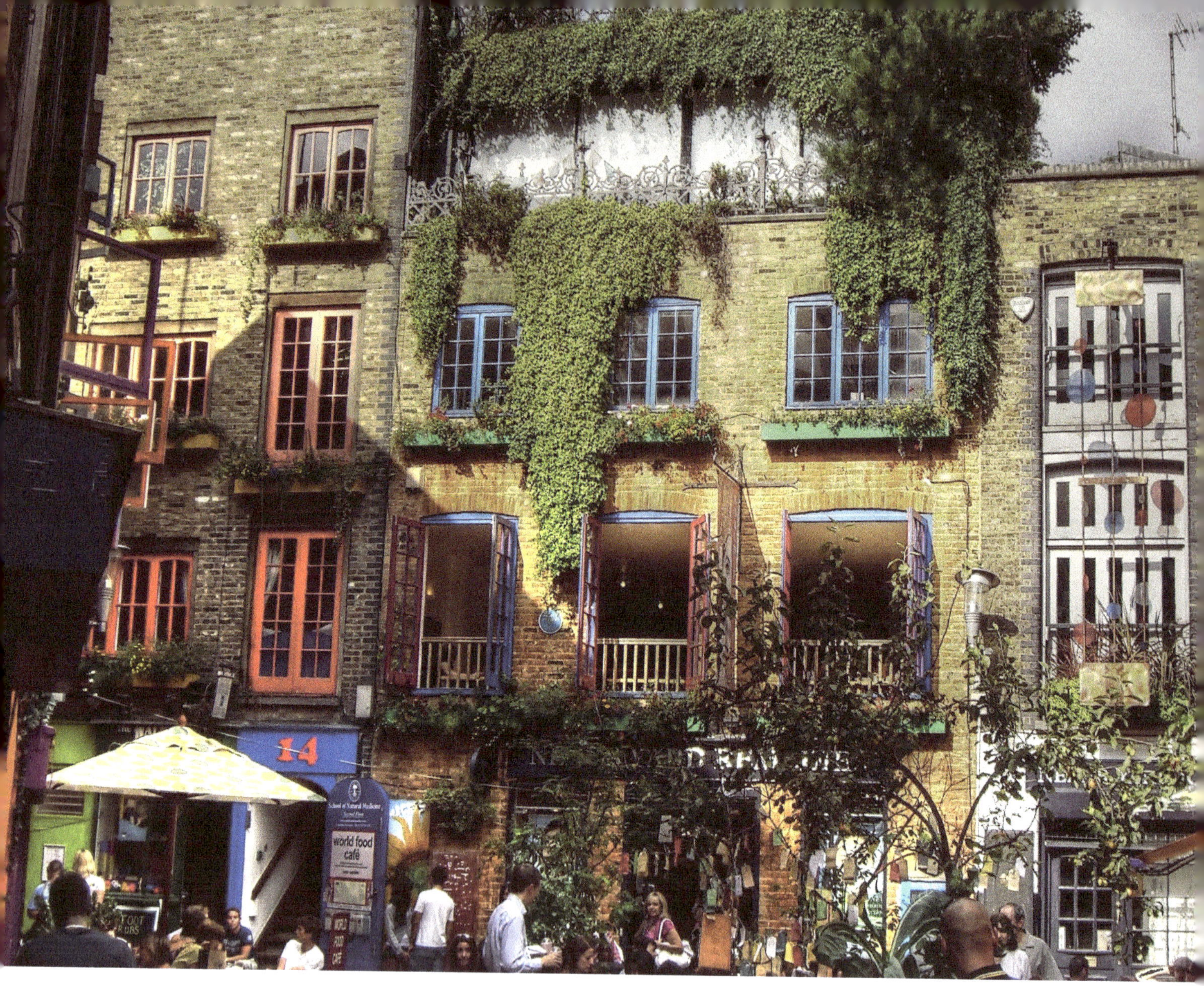

Neal's Yard

Photo by Mikel Ortega

Neal's Yard is a secluded courtyard in Covent Garden just minutes away from the main piazza. Neal's Yard is named after Thomas Neale, a 17th century entrepreneur. The area's focus is on healthy lifestyles: there is a vegan restaurant, a bakery, an organic beauty shop and a massage parlour. Homeslice, a highly-rated pizza place, can also be found here.

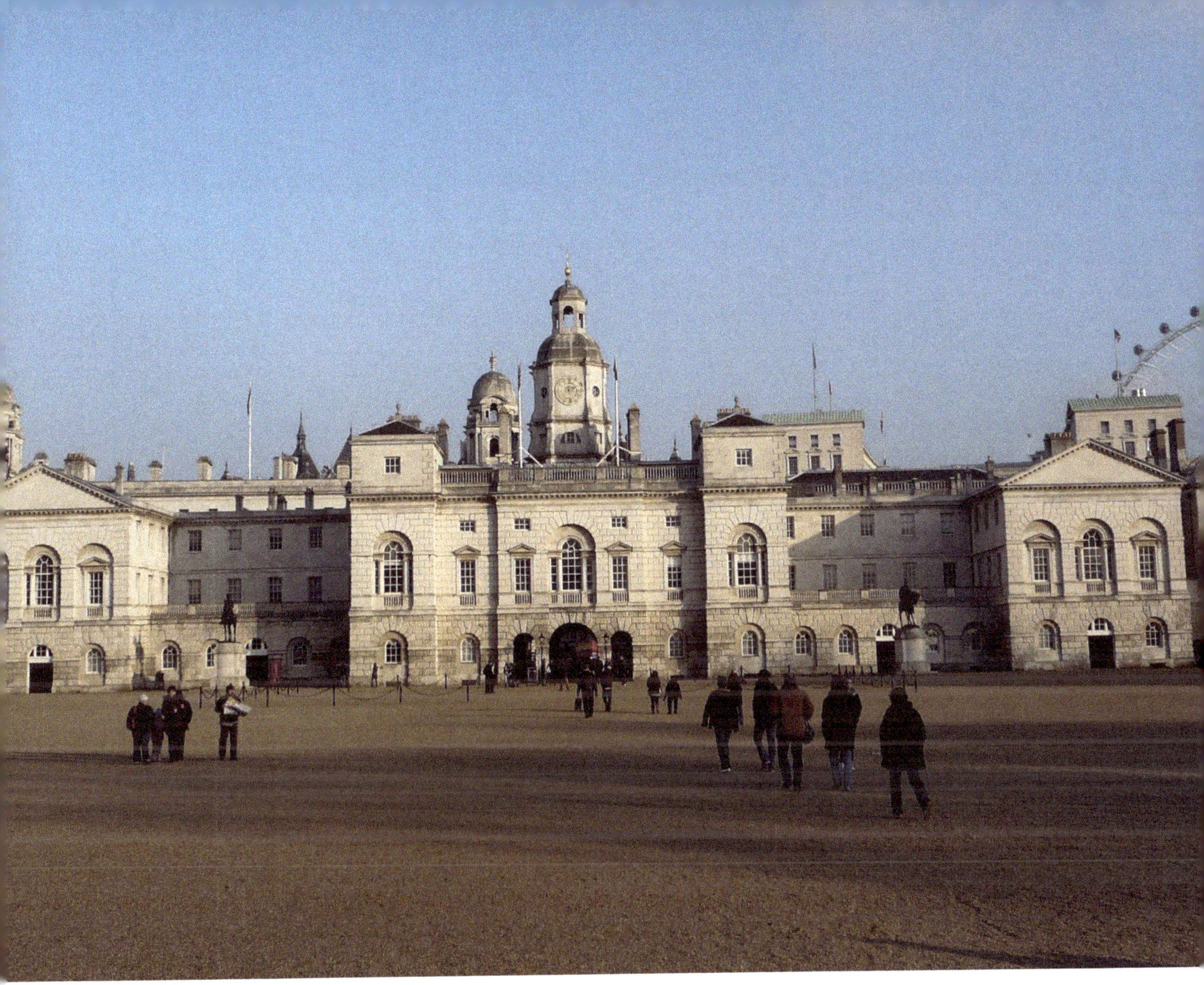

Horse Guards Parade

Photo by Ian Dick

Horse Guards Parade was originally the jousting ground of Whitehall Palace, but today is used to host events for ceremonial occasions such as the monarch's official birthday and the Trooping of the Colour ceremony. The white building at the centre of the image is Horse Guards dating from 1759 by William Kent - it is used by the military today.

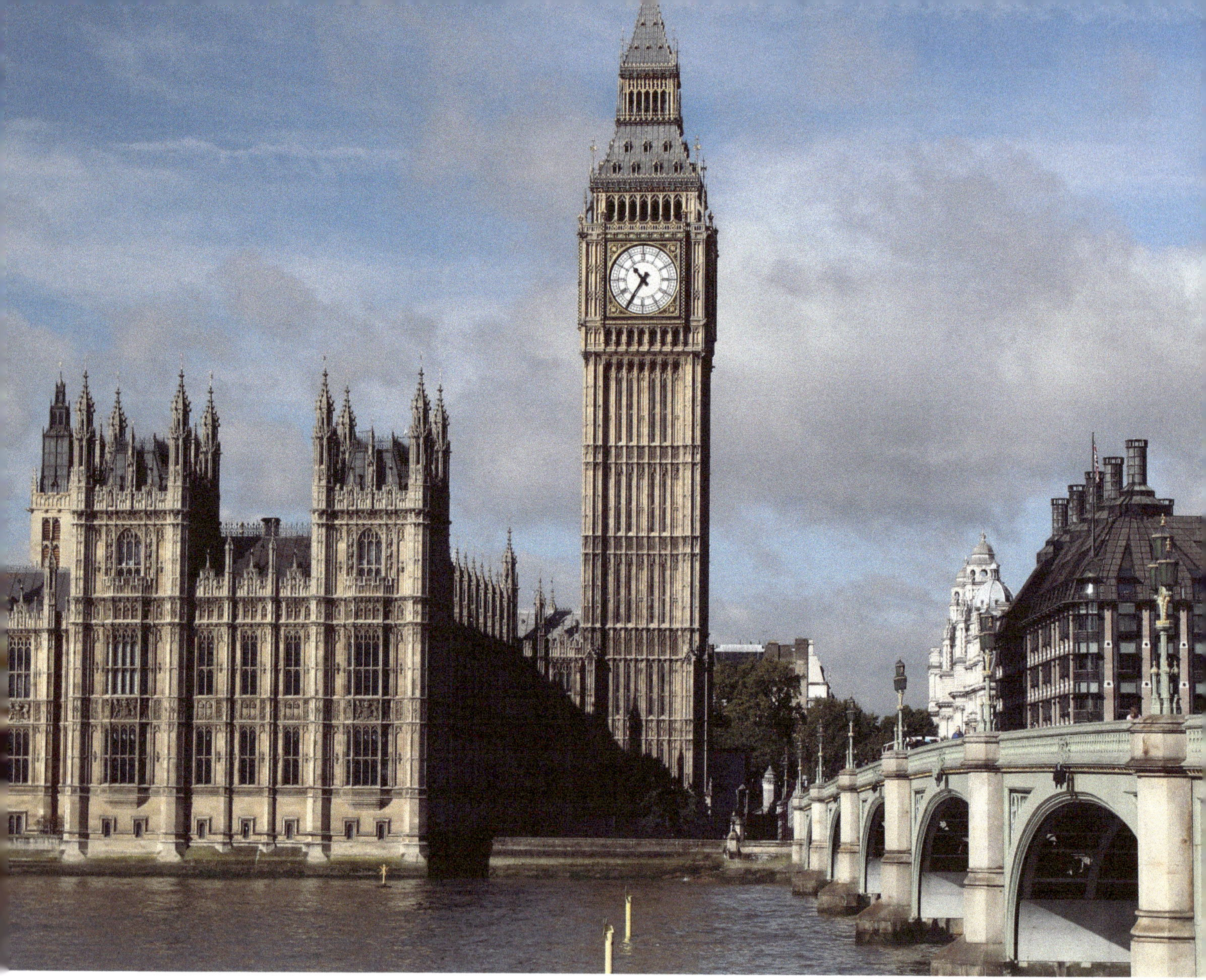

Palace of Westminster

Photo by Adam Asar

The Palace of Westminster, which dates mostly from the mid-19th century, is the meeting place of the House of Commons and the House of Lords, leading to it more commonly being called the Houses of Parliament. A royal palace has stood on this site since the 11th century; the building was last remodeled by architect Sir Charles Barry.

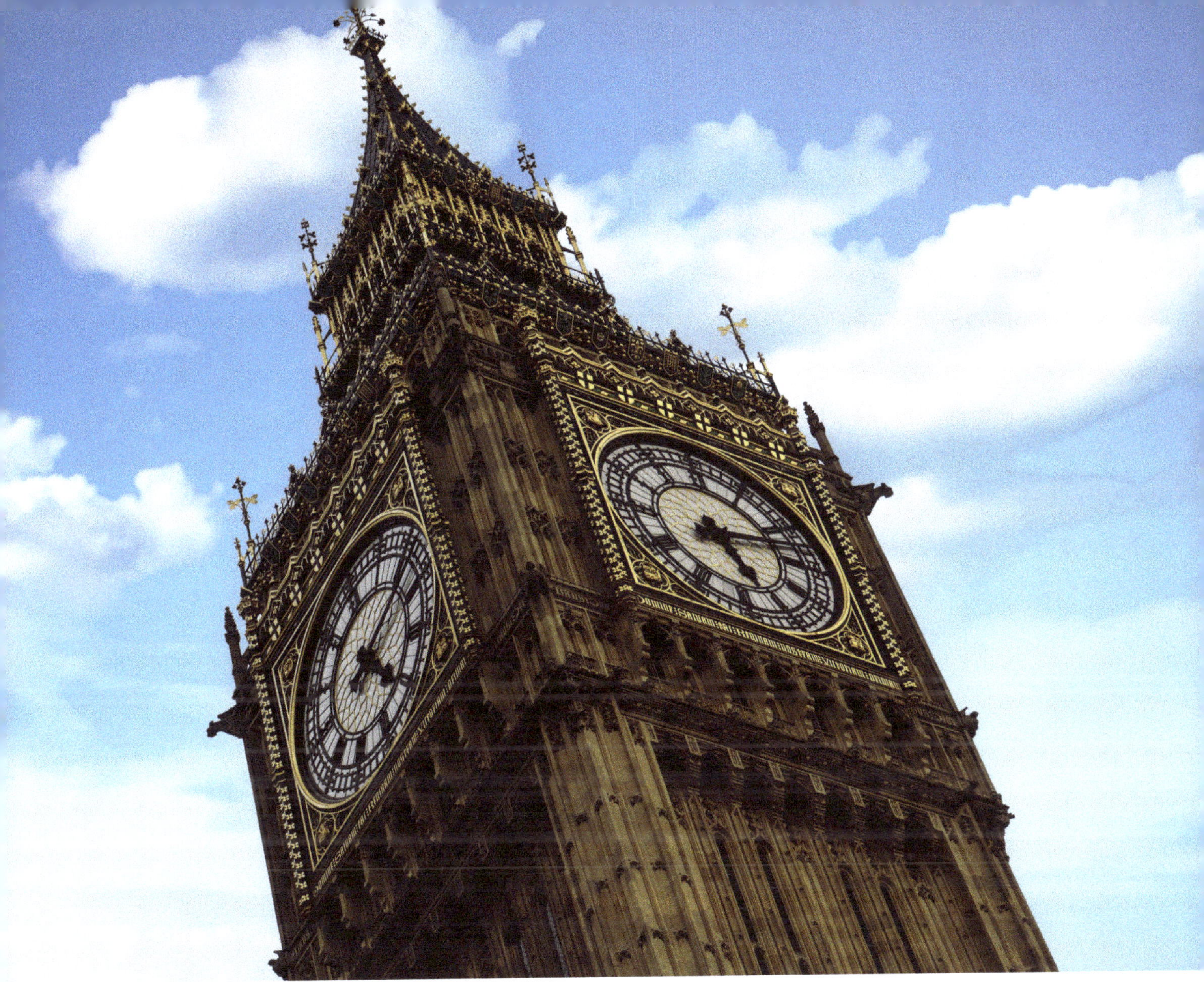

Photo by Norbert Reimer

Big Ben

The most famous part of the Palace of Westminster is the 315-foot tall Elizabeth Tower, more commonly known as Big Ben. Big Ben is actually the name of the bell inside the tower, which weighs over 13 tonnes. The tower's architect was Augustus Pugin, who also designed the interior of the palace - both are designed in a Gothic Revival style.

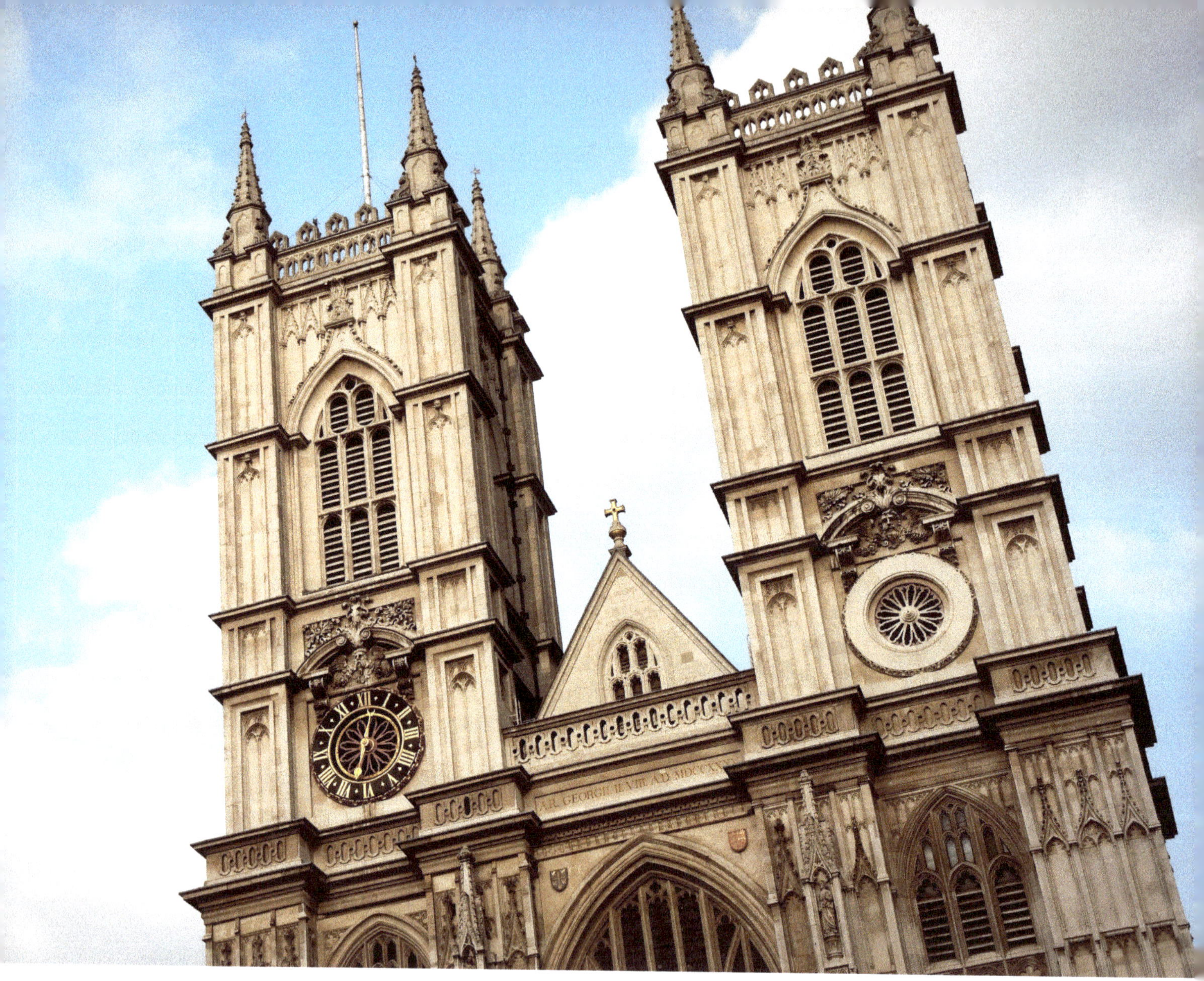

Westminster Abbey

Photo by Josh Hallett

There has been a church on this site since the 10th century, when Benedictine monks settled. The church was rebuilt in the early 11th century but the current church building was built between 1245 and 1745. The most recent extension is the Western Towers (pictured) by Nicholas Hawksmoor, which is now used as the "front" as the church.

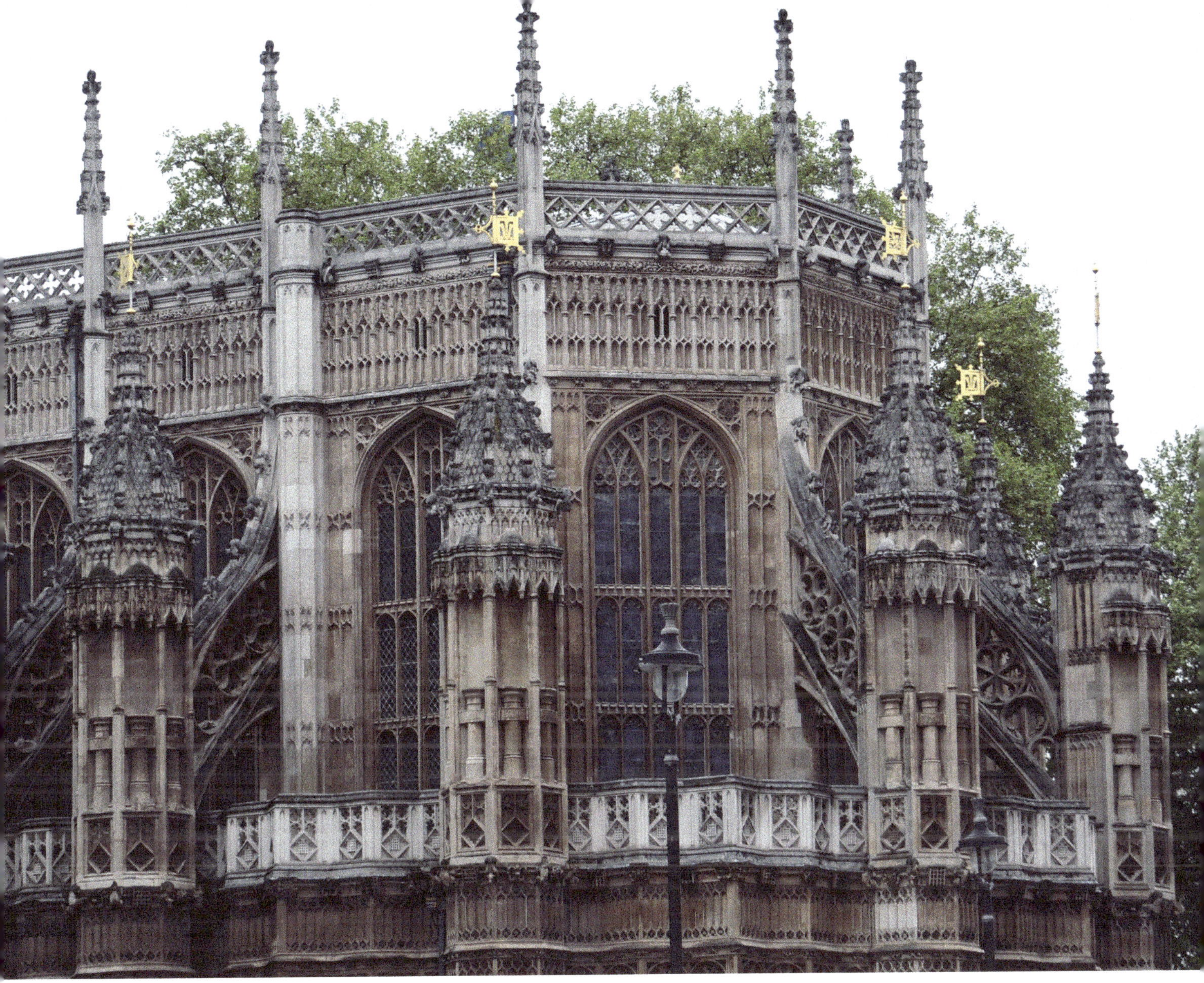

Photo by Aaron Bradley

Westminster Abbey

In 1066, King William I became the first monarch to be crowned inside the building, and since then almost every one of the country's coronations has taken place here - 38 in total, with the most recent being that of Queen Elizabeth II in 1953. The church is also used for royal weddings including that of Catherine Middleton and Prince William in 2011.

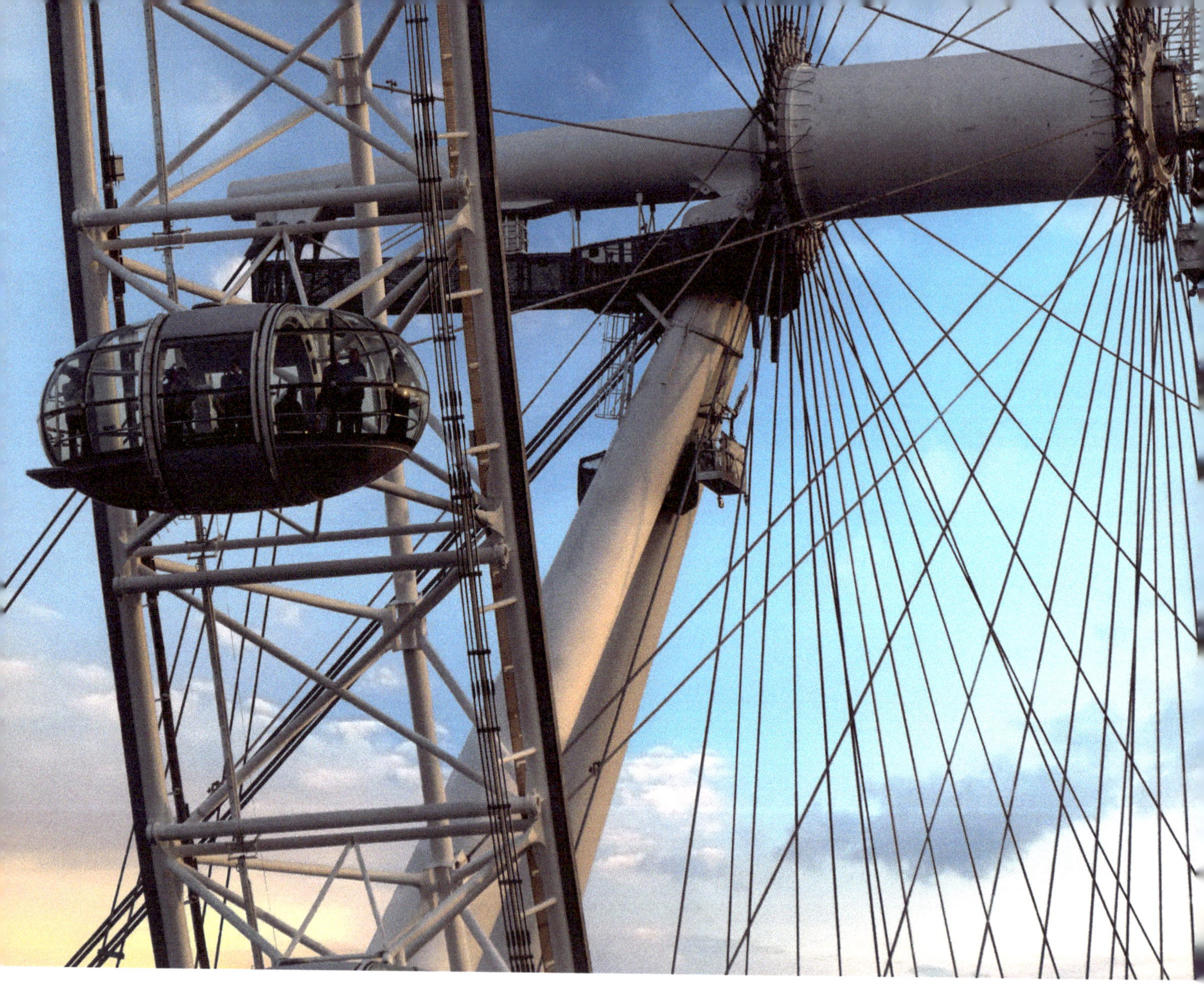

London Eye

Photo by Nobert Reimer

Originally known as the Millennium Wheel, this famous London landmark was only meant to be a temporary addition to London's skyline for 5 years to celebrate the new millennium. Today its 32 pods carry over 3.7 million passengers each year - one full revolution lasts approximately 30 minutes at a leisurely 0.6 miles per hour.

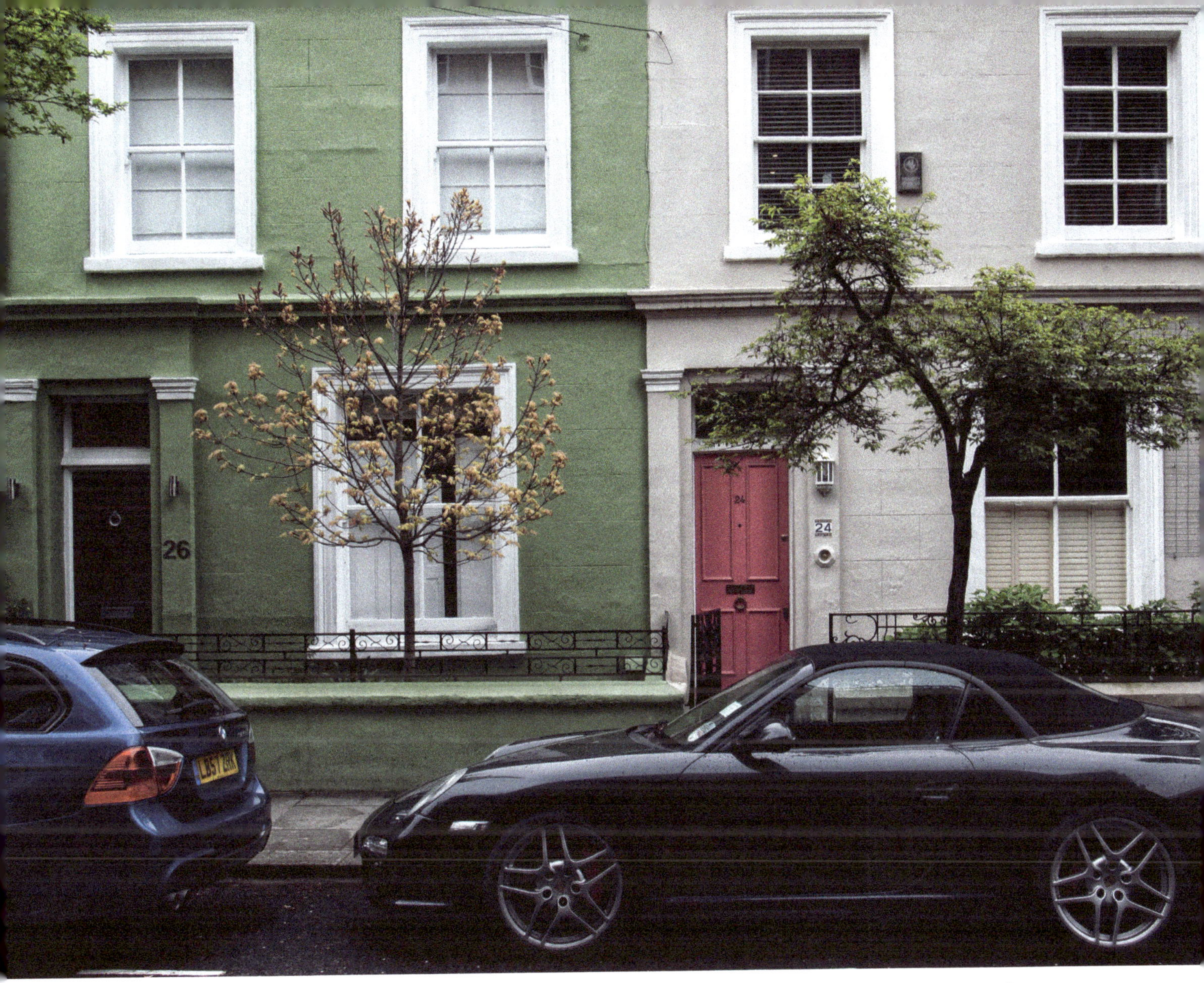

Photo by Raphael Chekroun

Notting Hill

Known for its colourful houses and posh residents, Notting Hill rose to fame in the 1999 film of the same name starring Hugh Grant and Julia Roberts. The area is known for the annual Notting Hill Carnival in August, and for Portobello Road Market - the world's largest antiques market, which takes place mainly on Saturdays.

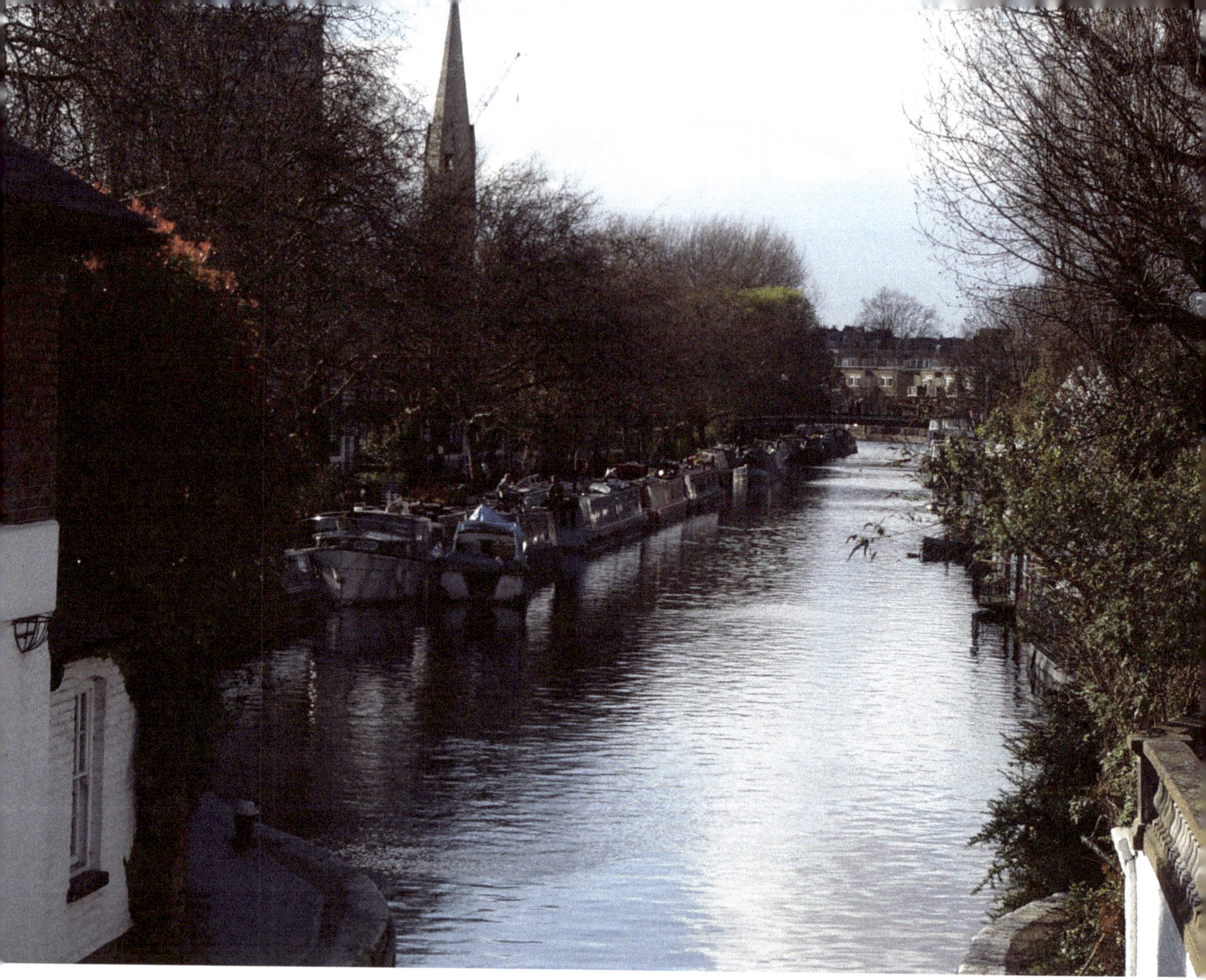

Little Venice

Photo by Clive G.

Little Venice was just a small village on the outskirts of London until the construction of the Paddington Canal in 1801. The Regent's Canal followed in 1812 and the area began to urbanise shortly afterwards. Today this area is known for its canal-side walkways, stucco houses and peaceful atmosphere despite being just minutes from bustling Edgware Road.

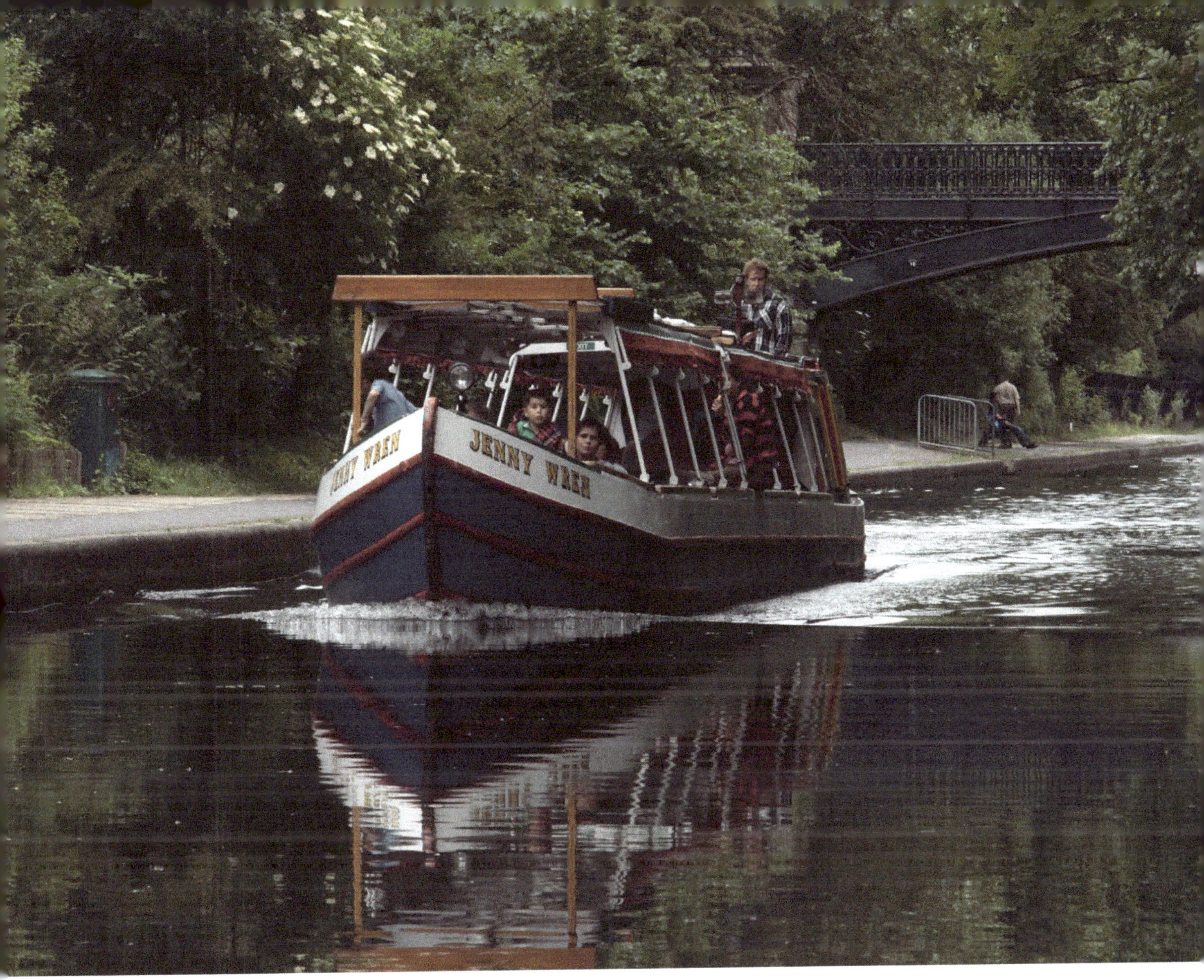

Photo by Mario Sanchez Prada

Grand Union Canal

The Grand Union Canal extends for 137 miles (220 km) from London to Birmingham. The Paddington arm of the canal runs through central London from Little Venice (Browning's Pool) to Hayes in West London - it runs for 27 miles and contains no locks. Today, the canal is mostly used for recreation, although it was initially used to transport goods.

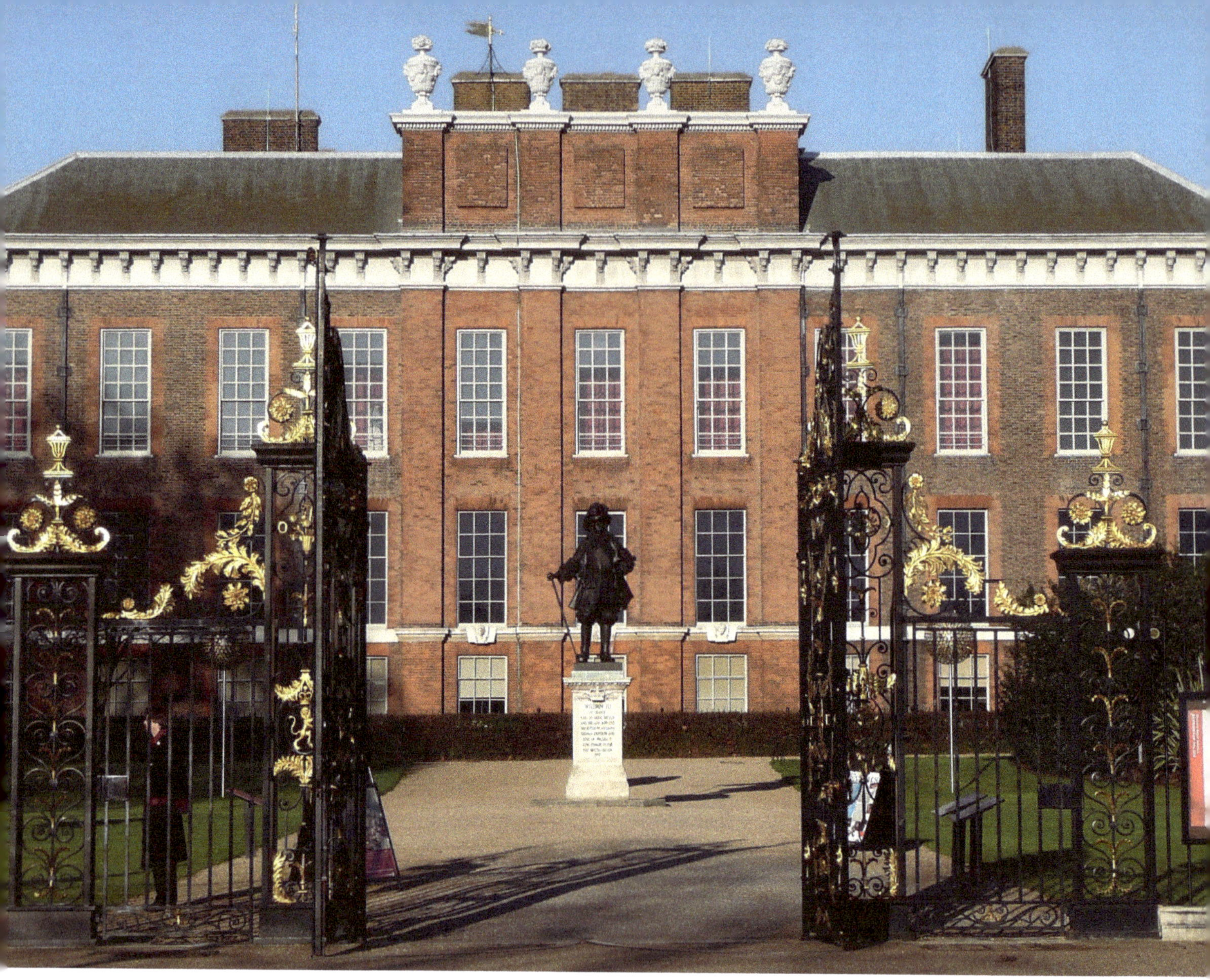

Kensington Palace

Photo by Herry Lawford

Kensington Palace was originally a mansion built in 1605 in the village of Kensington, which underwent significant expansion in the 18th century. More recently, the palace was home to Prince Charles and Diana from 1981 until 1997. Prince William and Kate Middleton live here with their children, along with Prince Harry and Megan Markle.

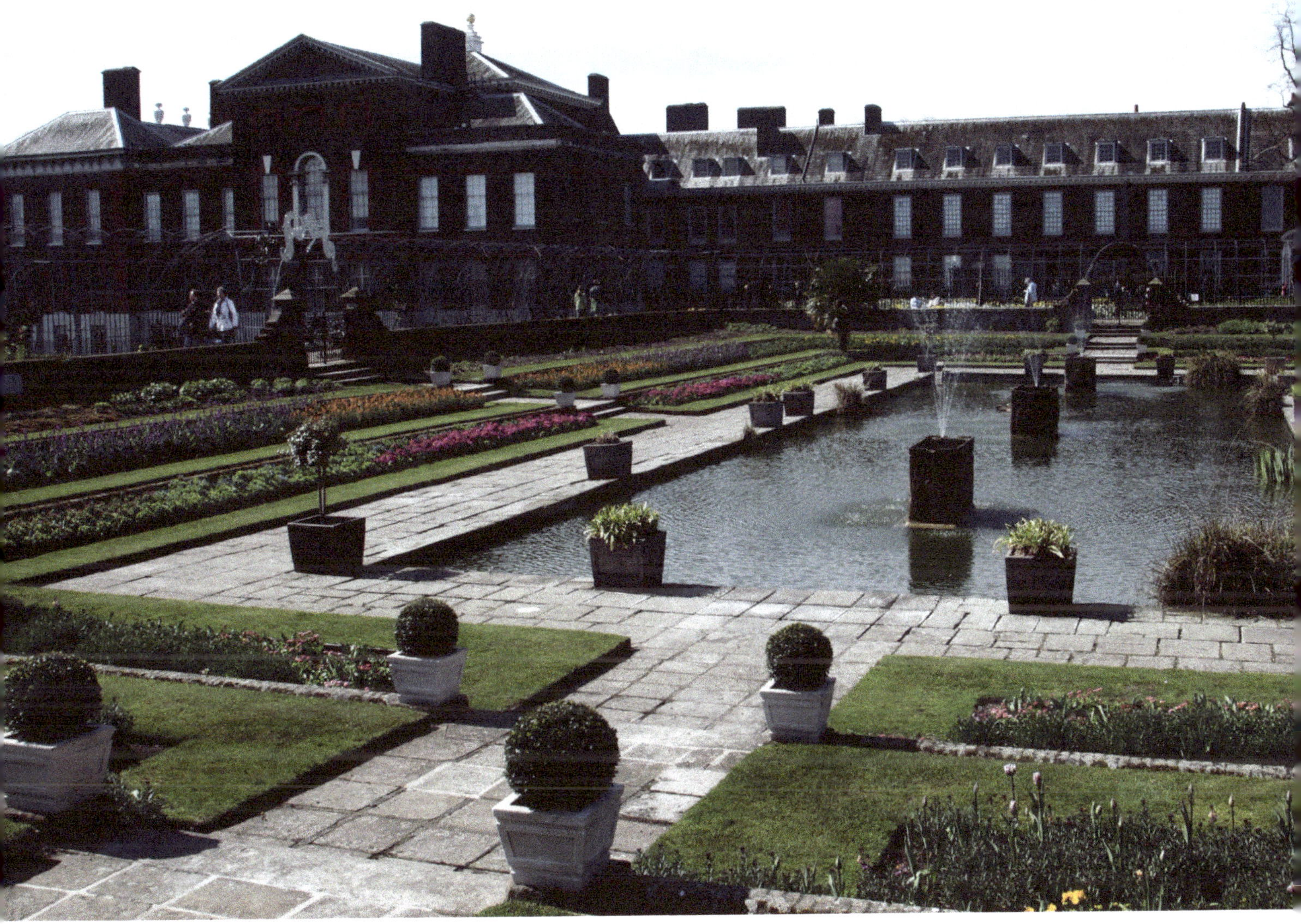

Photo by Herry Lawford

The Sunken Garden

Located in the non-ticketed area of the palace, and therefore publicly accessible, is the Sunken Garden. Also, known as a Dutch Garden, the current design dates from 1908. The walkways around the garden have arched trees with spots to spot and take photos, as well as benches to relax on – in the evening, fairy lights are switched on.

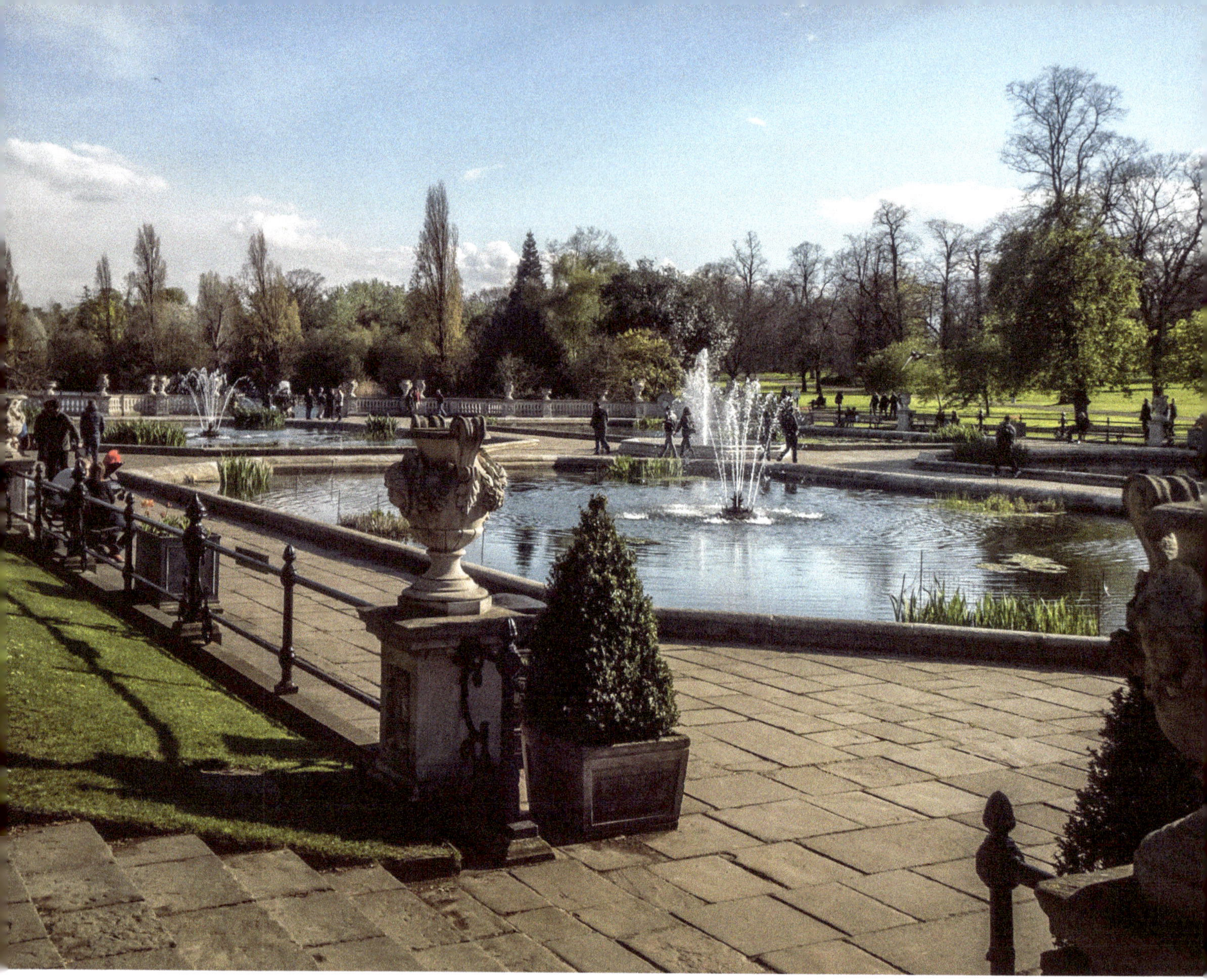

Italian Water Gardens

Photo by Garry Knight

The Italian Water Gardens are located in the northeast portion of Kensington Gardens. The gardens were inspired by Osborne House on the Isle of Wight. Prince Albert visited these gardens and sought to recreate them in London as a present to his wife, Queen Victoria - the gardens were created in the 1860s and were designed by James Pennethorne.

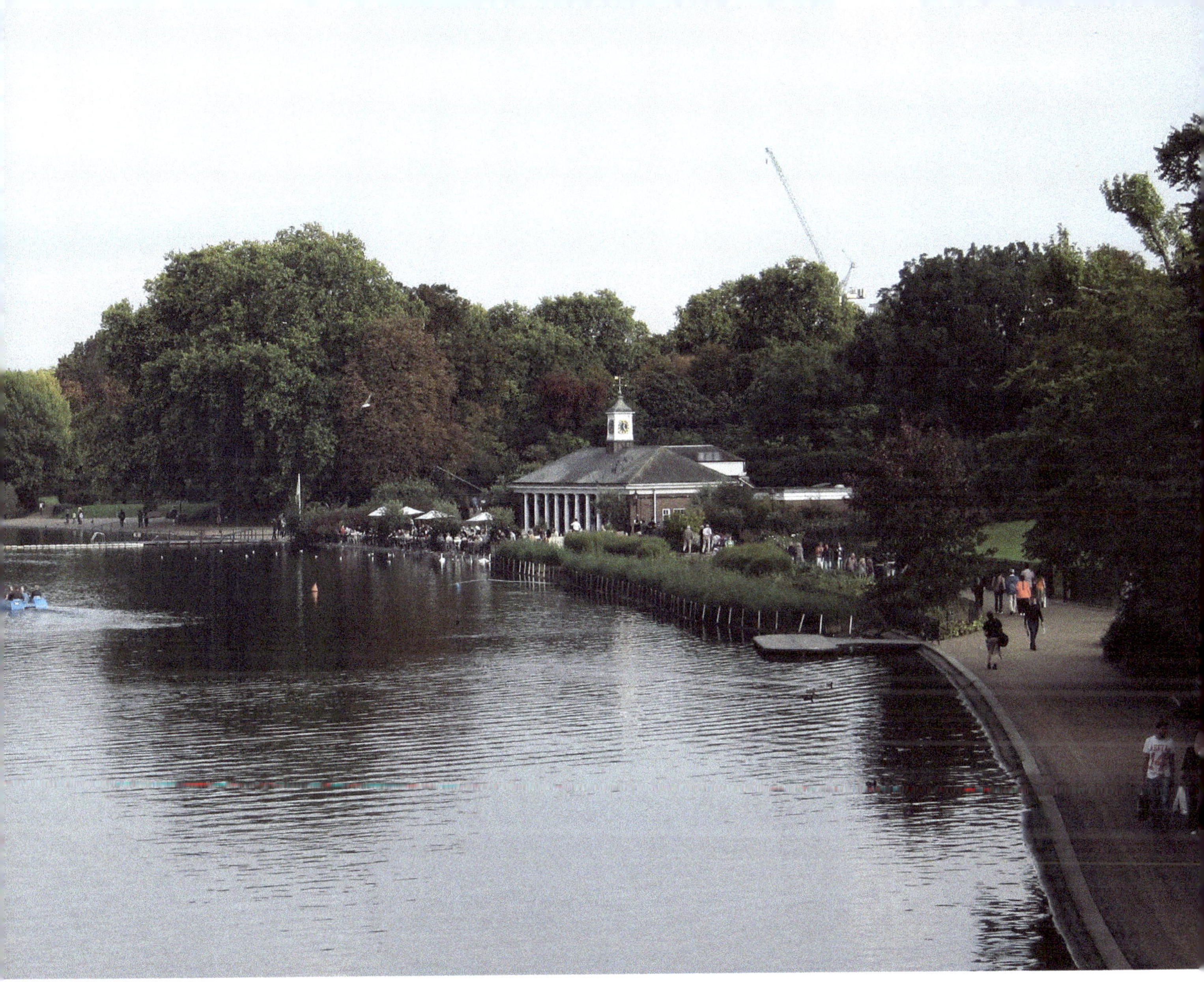

Photo by Alan Stanton

The Serpentine

The Serpentine is the name of the large man-made lake in the centre of Hyde Park. The lake spans across 40 acres and was created in 1730 under the instruction of Queen Caroline, wife of King George II. The lake's name is thought to derive from its snake-like shape. Today the lake features an open-air lido and boats available for recreational use.

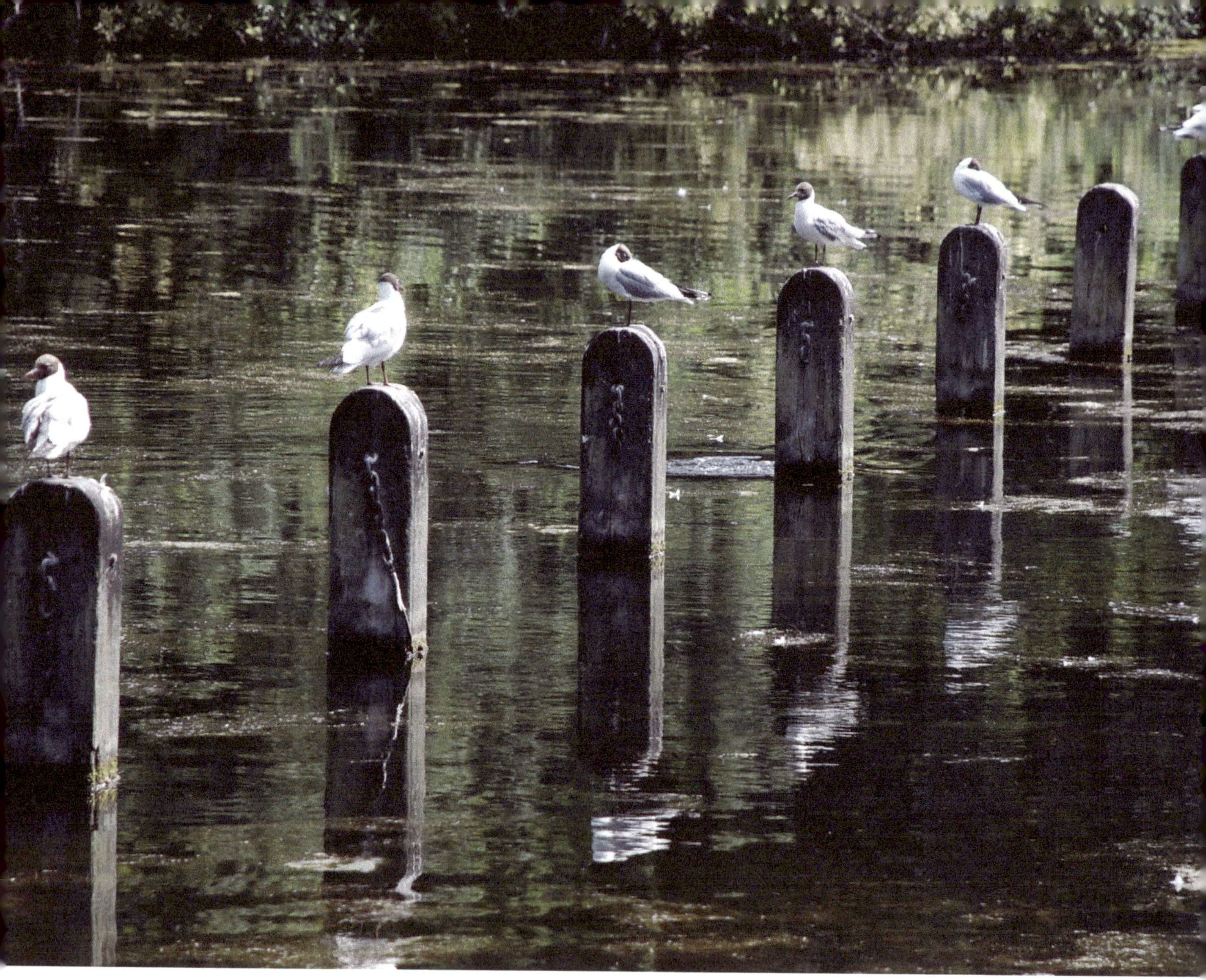

The Long Water

Photo by Maurits Ruis

Whereas The Serpentine is the name of the body of water in Hyde Park, at Kensington Gardens the continuation of the lake is known as The Long Water. If you explore the gardens you may come across wildfowl such as the black-headed gulls pictured, and even beautiful parakeets - no-one seems to know quite how they got here!

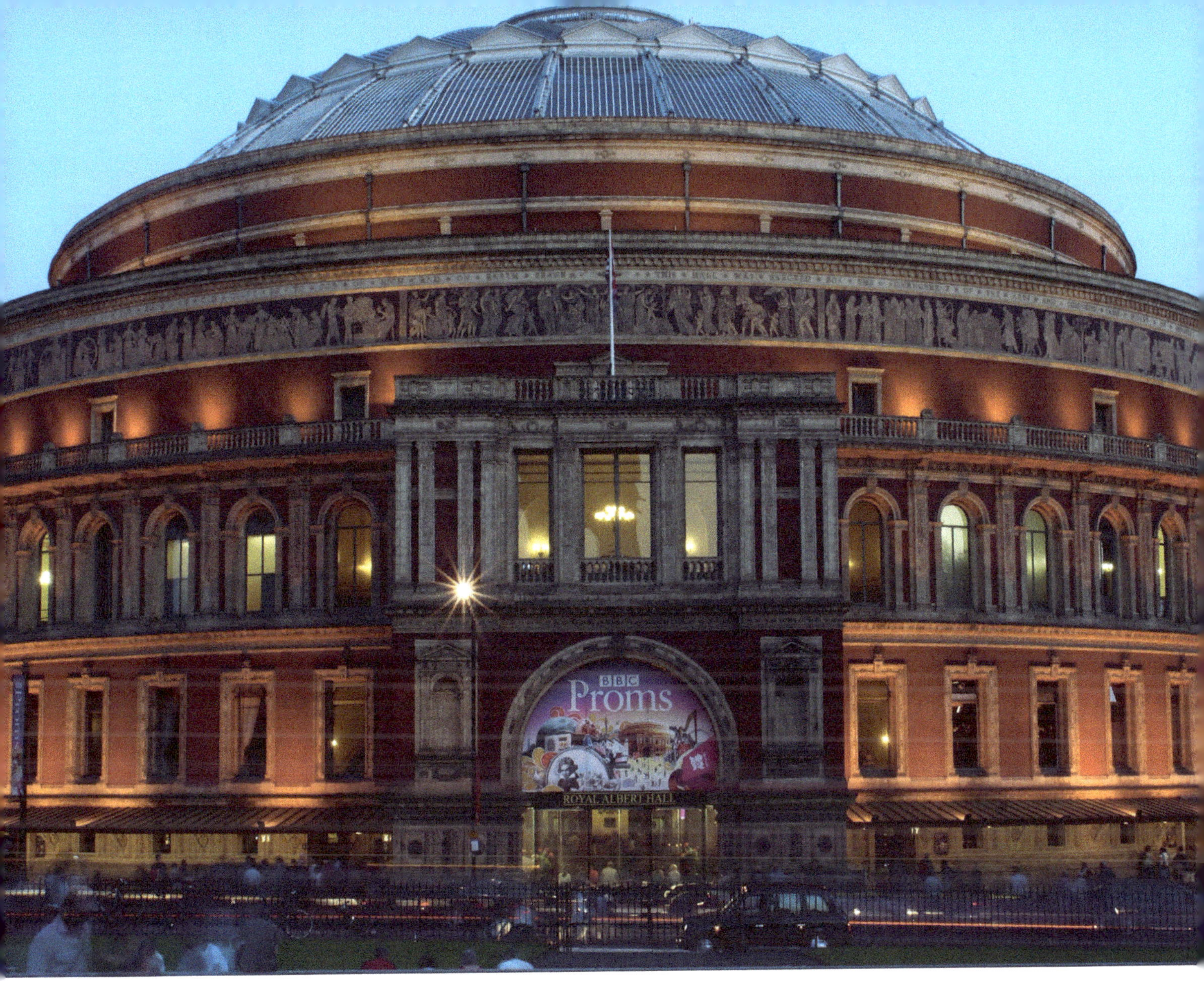

Photo by Paul Hudson

Royal Albert Hall

At the south of Kensington Gardens is the beautiful RAH. This arts venue is located on land planned by Prince Albert to become a cultural quarter which became nicknamed "Albertopolis". Unfortunately, Albert died before this vision was realised but this concert venue stands as a memorial to him. The RAH hosts the classical BBC Proms each summer.

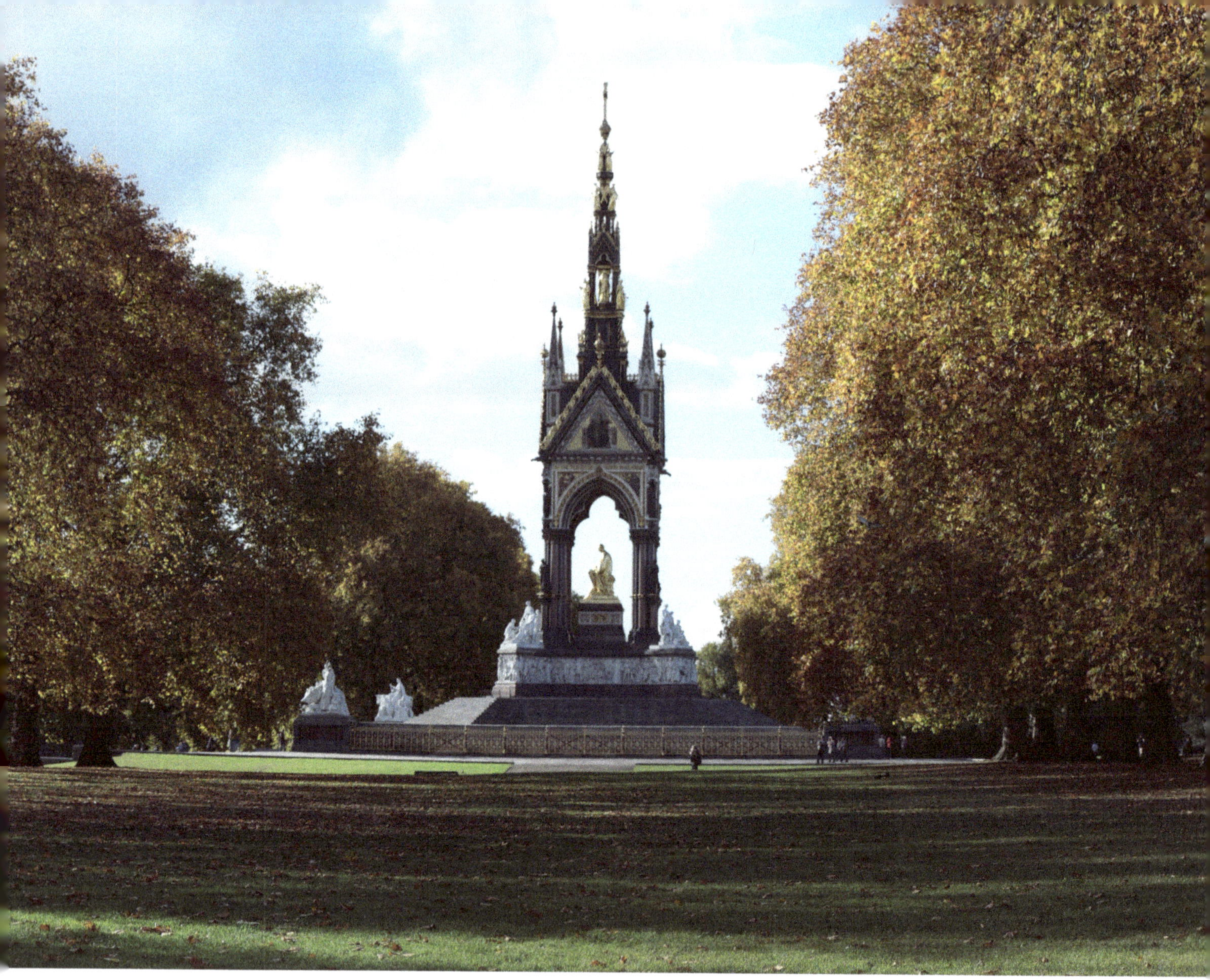

Albert Memorial

Photo by Nicolas de Camaret

Standing opposite the main entrance to the Royal Albert Hall in Kensington Gardens is the Albert Memorial. It was designed by Sir George Gilbert Scott in a Gothic Revival style and was unveiled in 1872. The statue of Albert looking towards Albertopolis in the centre was added four years later.

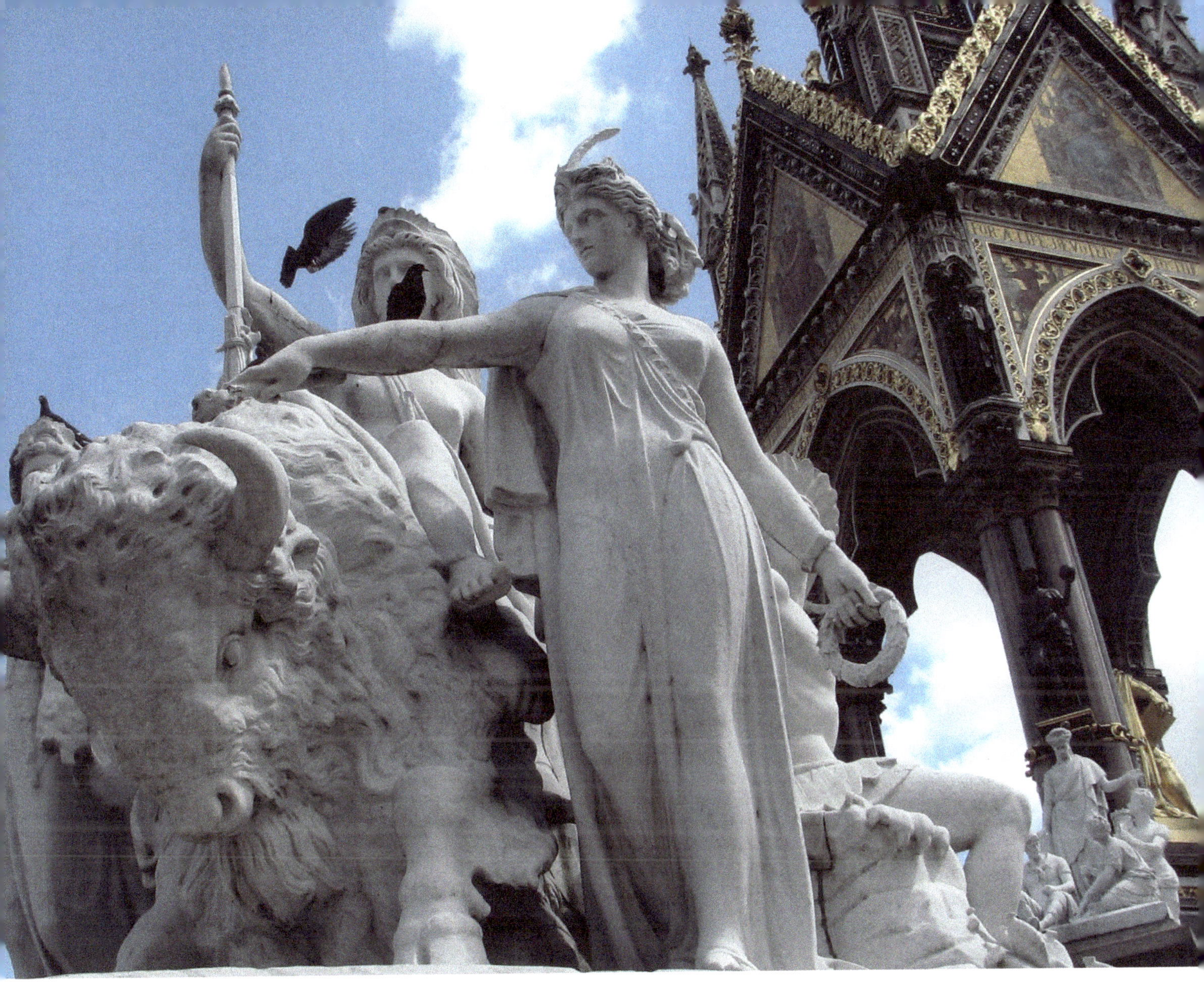

Photo by Yaffa Phillips

Albert Memorial

The memorial features statues celebrating Victorian industry – agriculture, commerce, engineering and manufacturing. On the outer four corners, there are four more sets of statues for four continents: Europe, Africa, Asia and the Americas (pictured). The memorial is as much about Albert as it is about the dominance of the British empire and its success.

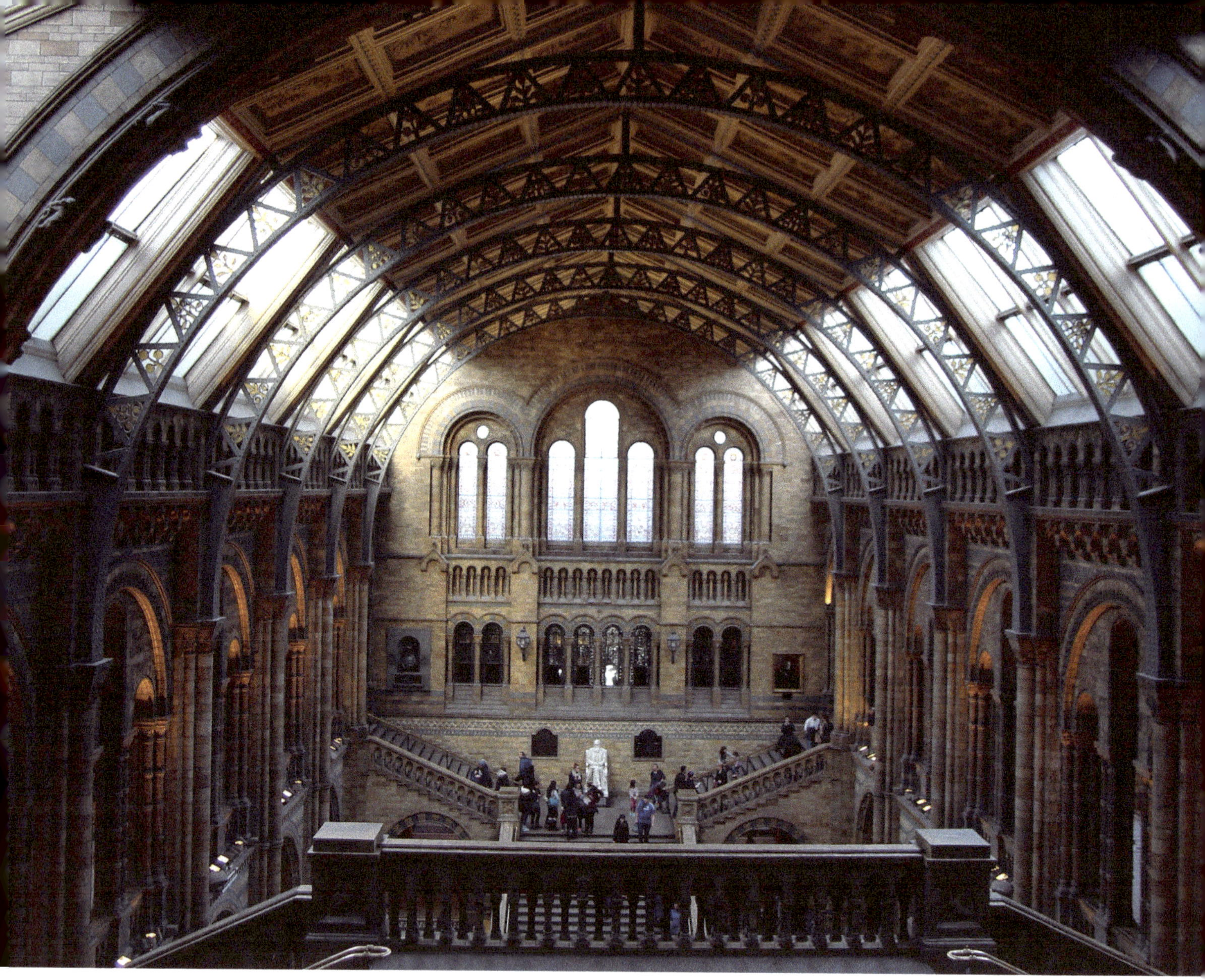

Natural History Museum

Photo by Kathryn Yengel

This gigantic museum houses 80 million items covering five main themes: plants, insects, minerals, fossils and animals. The building the NHM is housed in was designed by Alfred Waterhouse in a Romanesque style with terracotta tiles both inside and out. The building's architecture had led to the museum being described as a "cathedral of nature".

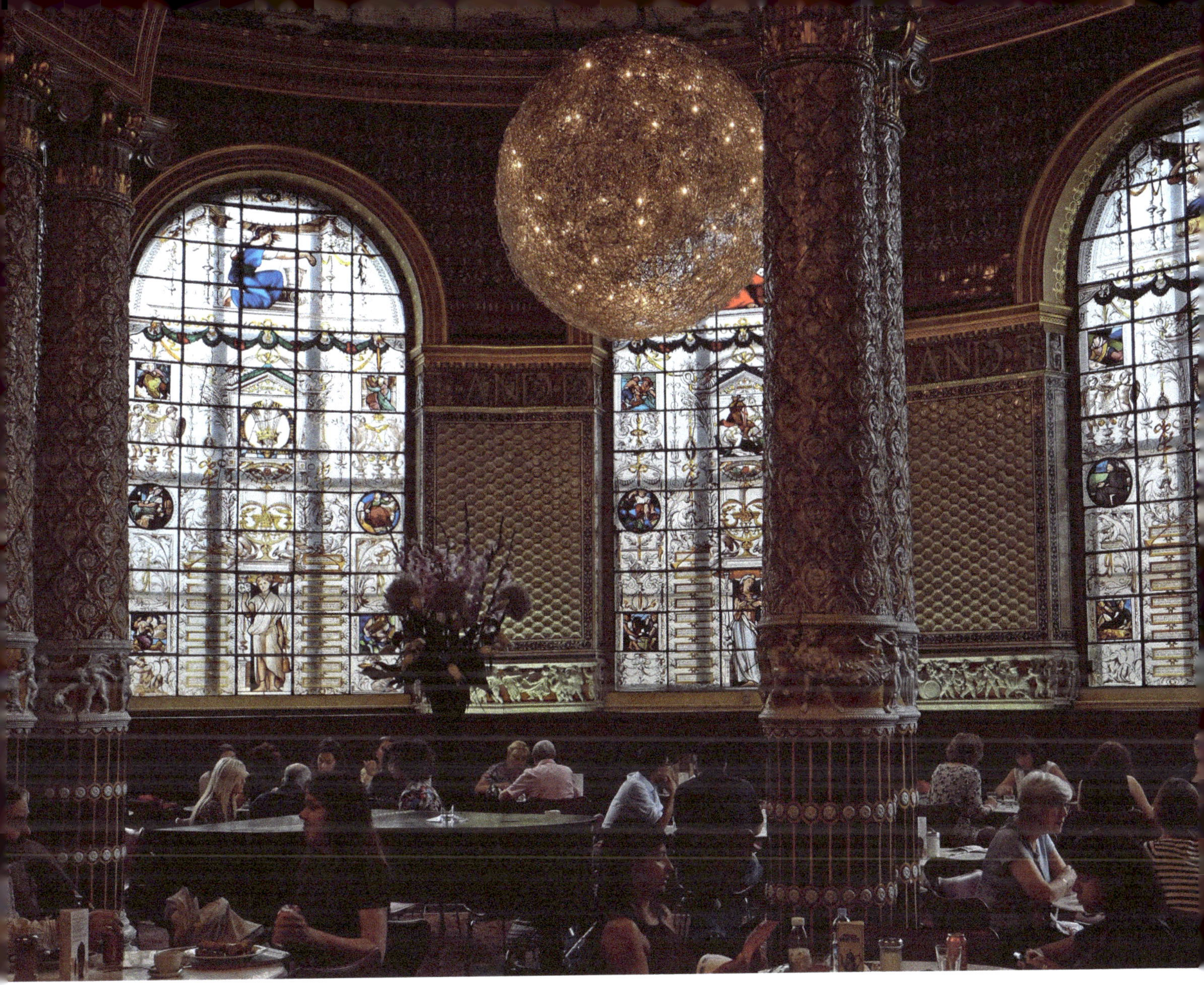

Photo by Eric Huybrechts

Victoria & Albert Museum

The Victoria & Albert Museum (V&A) was established in 1852 as the Museum of Manufactures at Marlborough House near Buckingham Palace. The collection later moved to Somerset House, and in 1857 it opened as the South Kensington Museum on its current site. Today it is the largest art and design museum in the world. The cafe is pictured above.

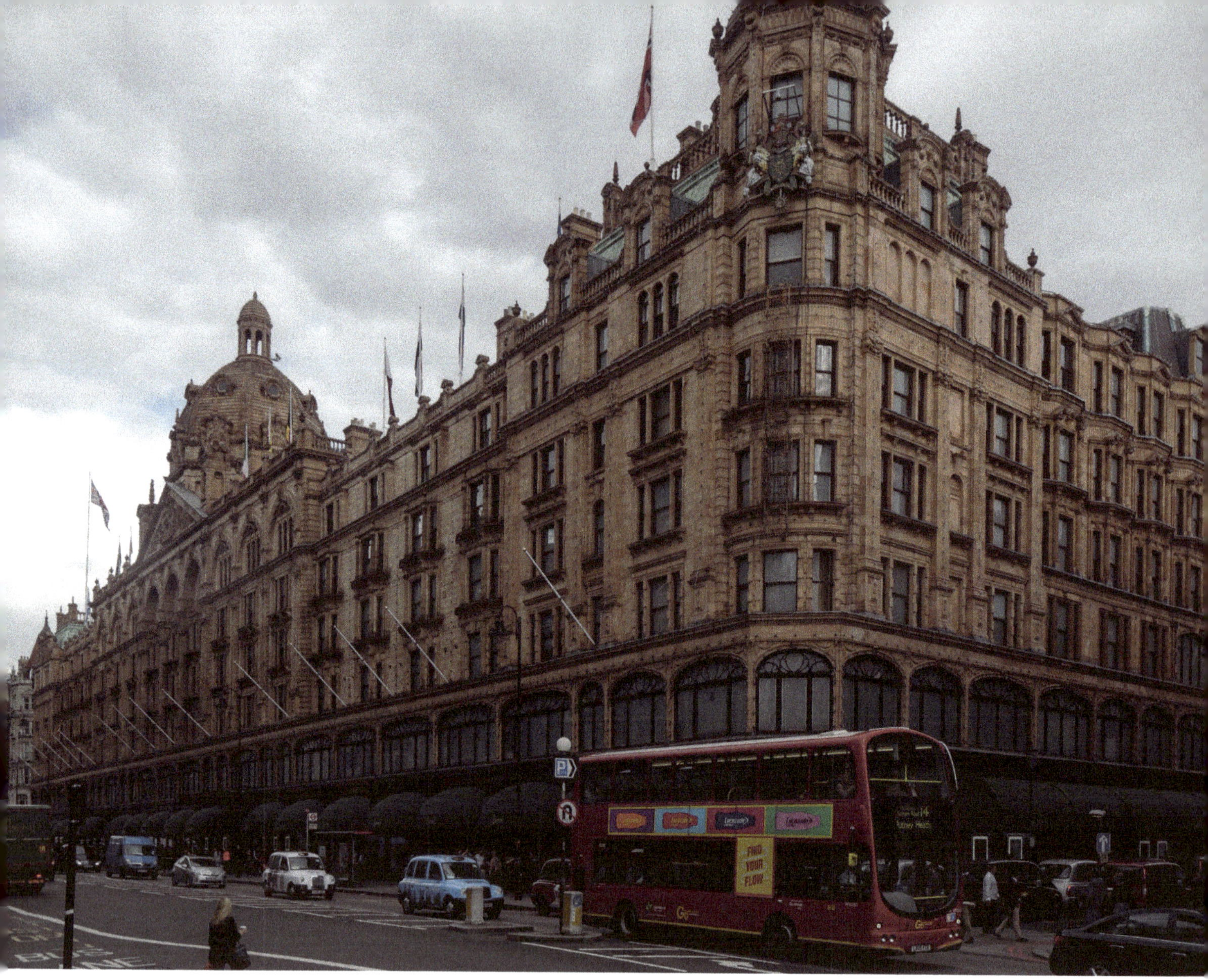

Harrods

Photo by Xiquinho Silva

Harrods was established by Charles Henry Harrod in 1824 and moved to its current site in 1849. Today, Harrods is the biggest department store in Europe, with retail space of 1 million ft2 (90,000 m2). The shop was previously owned by Mohammed Al Fayed, whose son Dodi Fayed dated Diana Spencer after her divorce with Prince Charles.

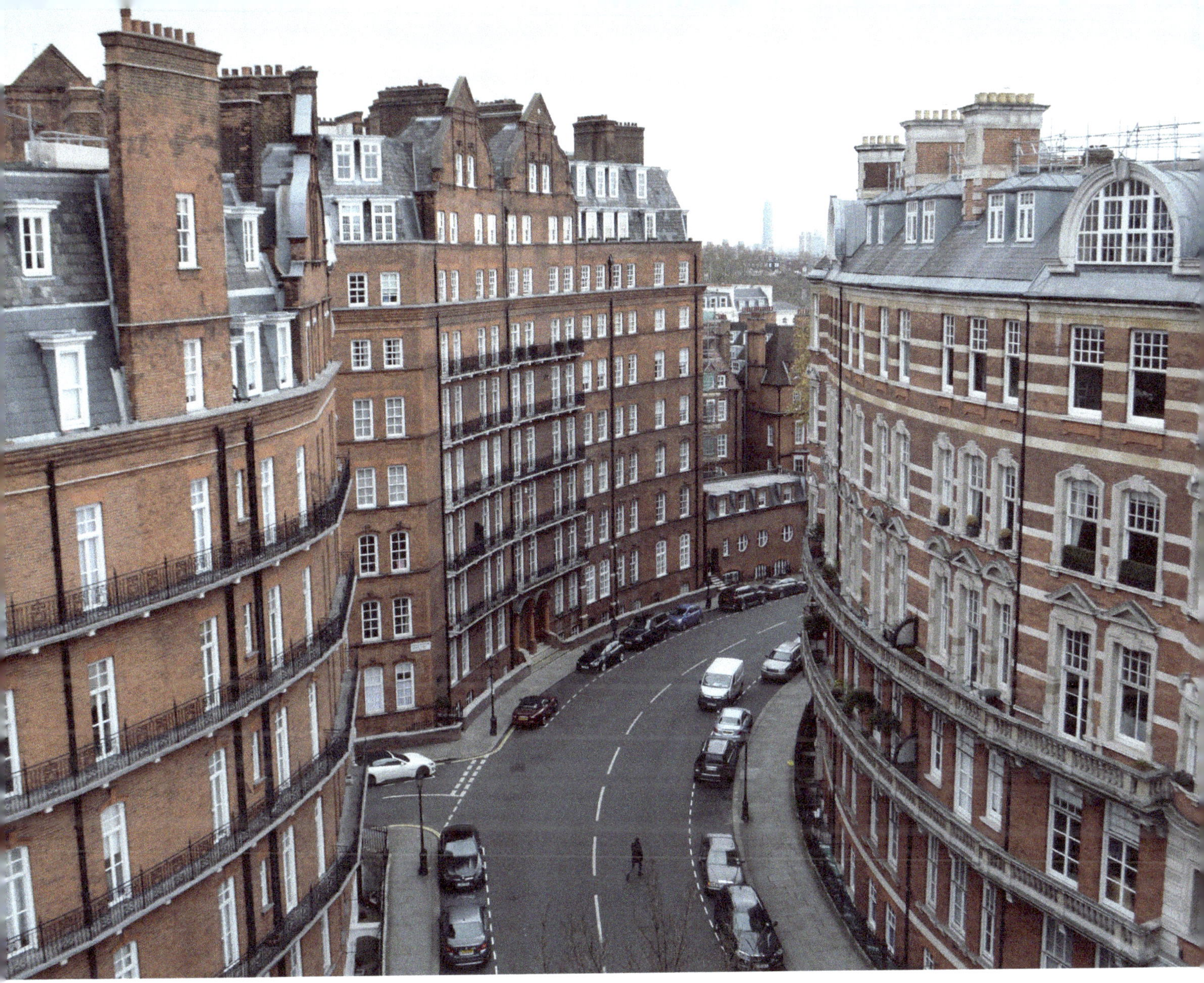

Photo by Matt Brown

Kensington Gore

Kensington Gore is lined with Victorian red-brick mansion blocks built when land in areas fashionable with the rich was scarce. Flats were, however, unpopular as they were seen as housing for the poorer classes and foreigners. Mansion blocks were built as luxury homes with several bedrooms, high ceilings, spacious interiors and often marble hallways.

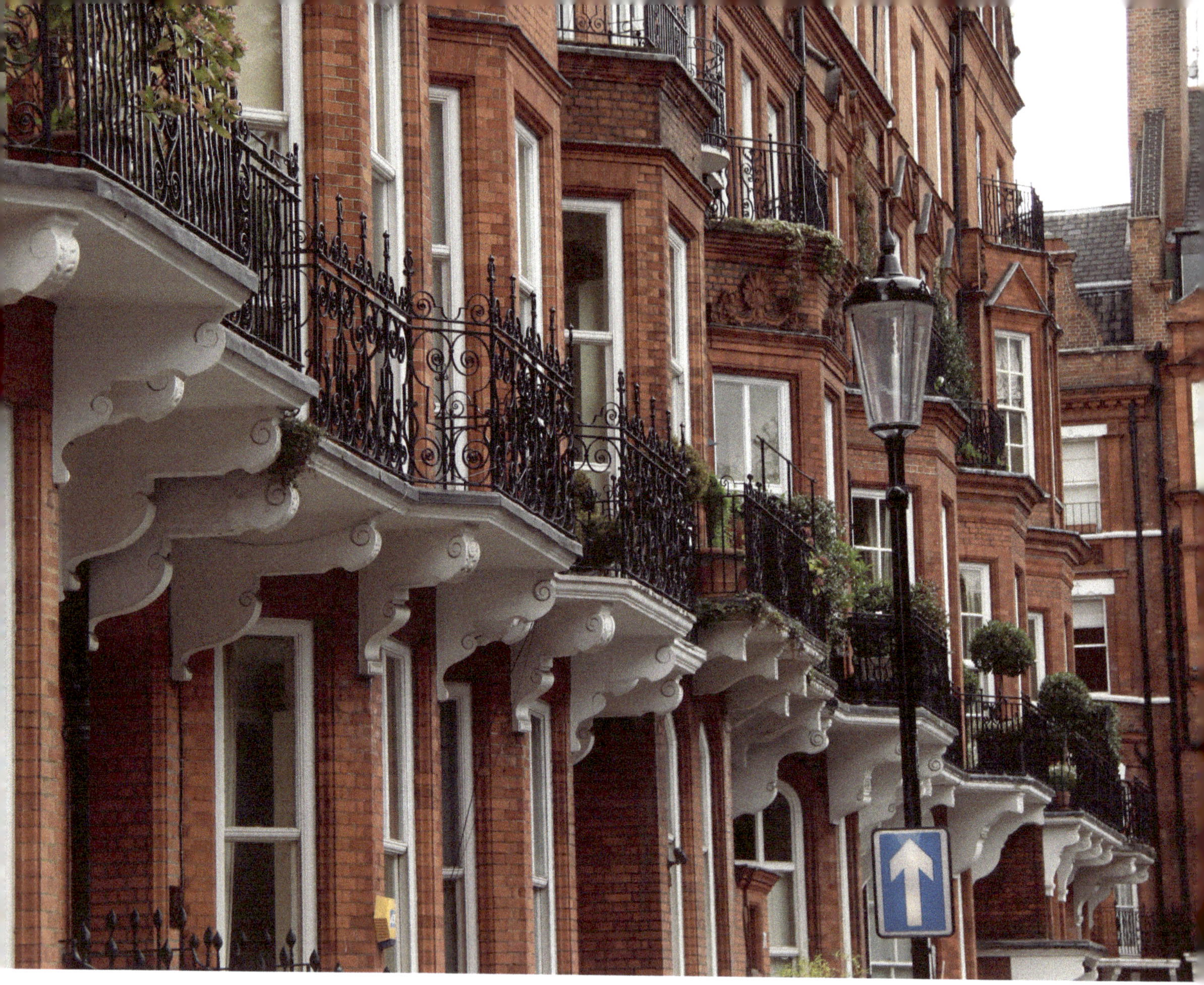

Chelsea

Photo by Cristian Bortes

Chelsea is another of London's most affluent areas to live in. Sandwiched between Knightsbridge, Belgravia and the River Thames, this part of London has a village-like feel to its streets. In the 19th century, Chelsea was known as the artist's district when painters such as J. M. W. Turner and Dante Gabriel Rossetti called this place home.

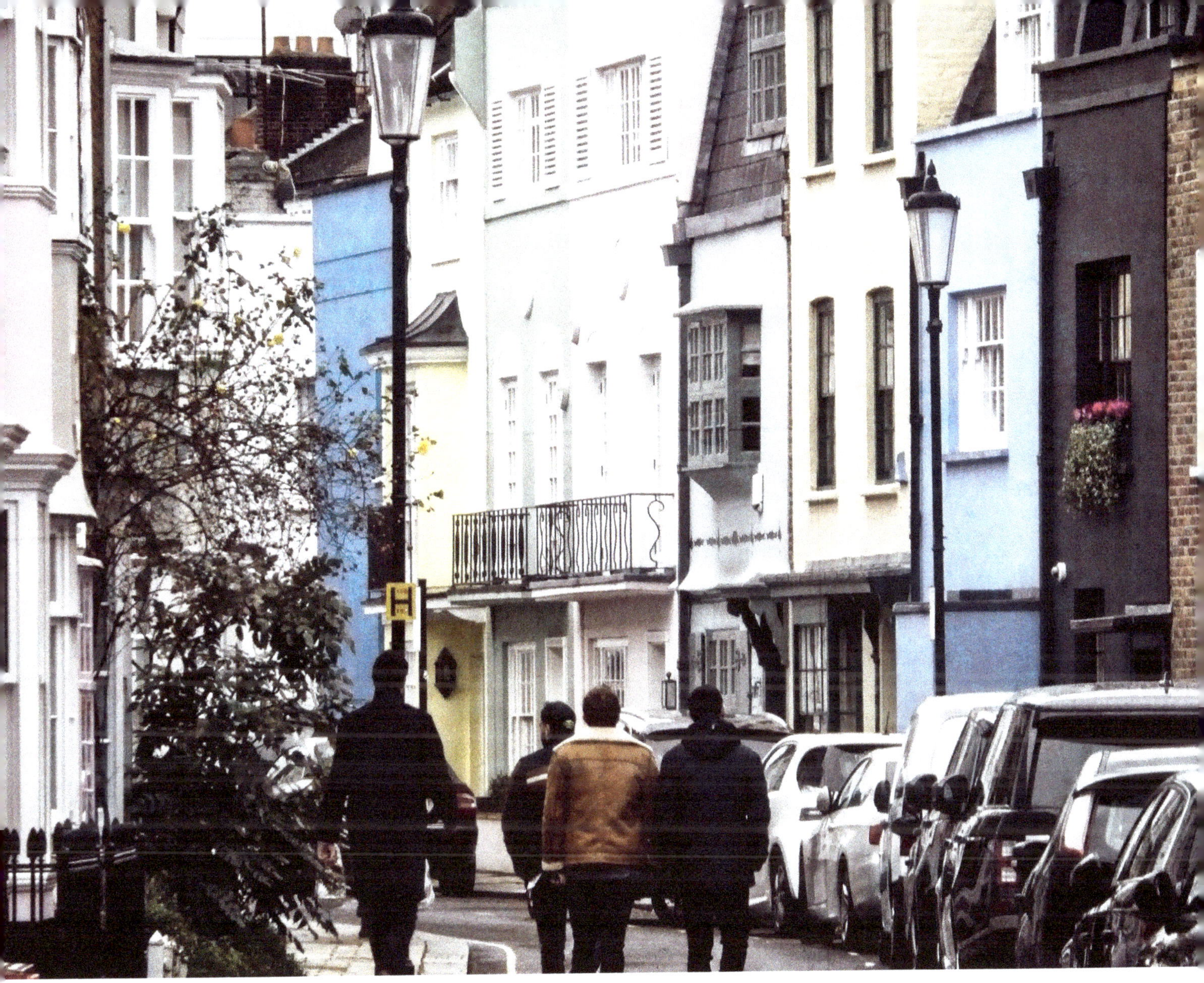

Photo by Garry Knight

Chelsea

Other notable Chelsea residents have included Oscar Wilde, T. S. Eliot and Agatha Christie. Every May since 1912, the Chelsea Flower Show has taken place in the grounds of the Royal Hospital Chelsea - a wide variety of garden styles are exhibited to the paying public. Pictured is Godfrey Street - one of Chelsea's most picturesque residential roads.

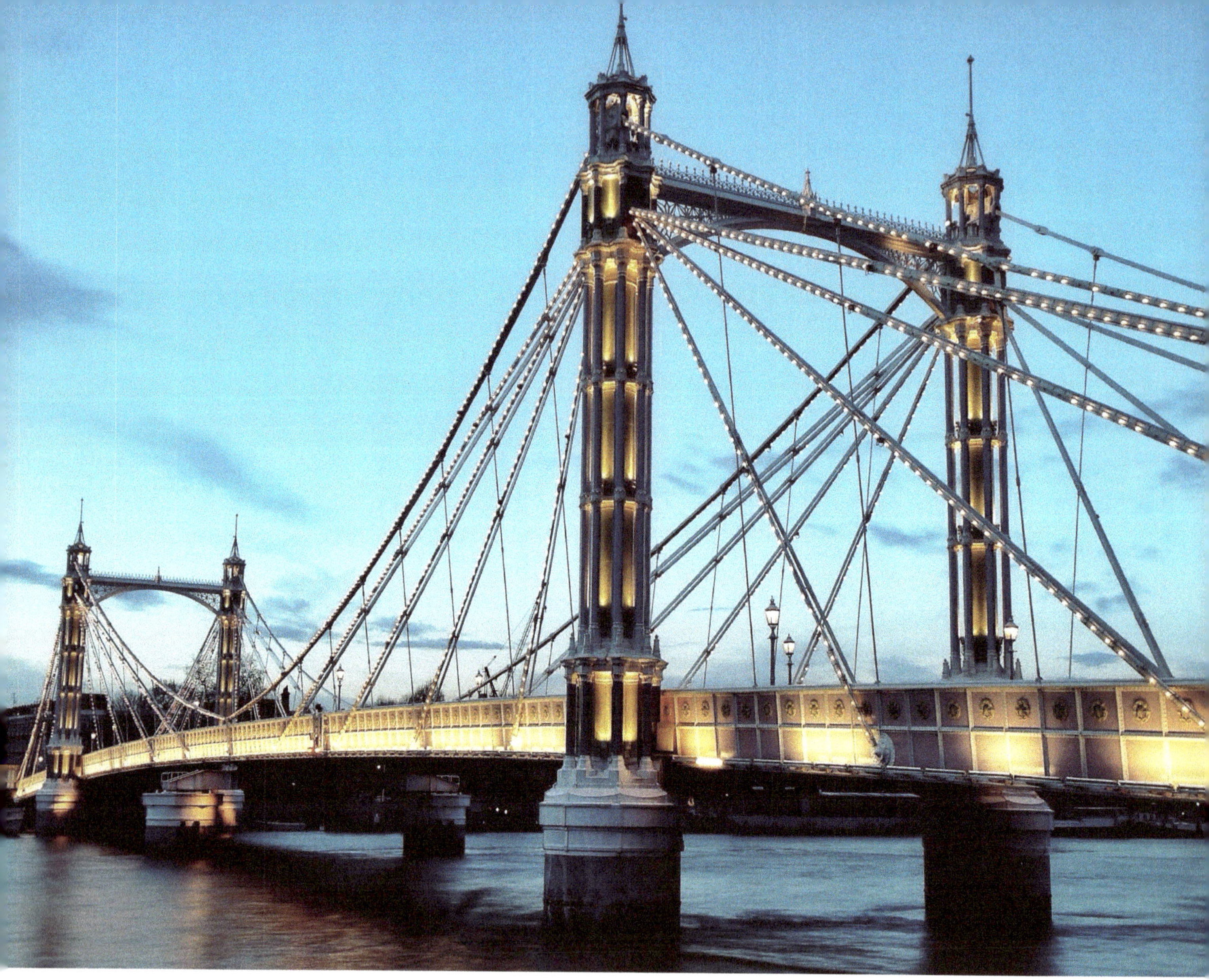

Albert Bridge

Photo by Mike Rolls

The Albert Bridge crosses the River Thames in south-west London and connects Chelsea with Battersea. The bridge was initially built in 1873, though it was modified in the 1880s and again in the 1970s. The bridge is nicknamed the "Trembling Lady" due to the vibrations experienced when crossed by too many pedestrians at the same time.

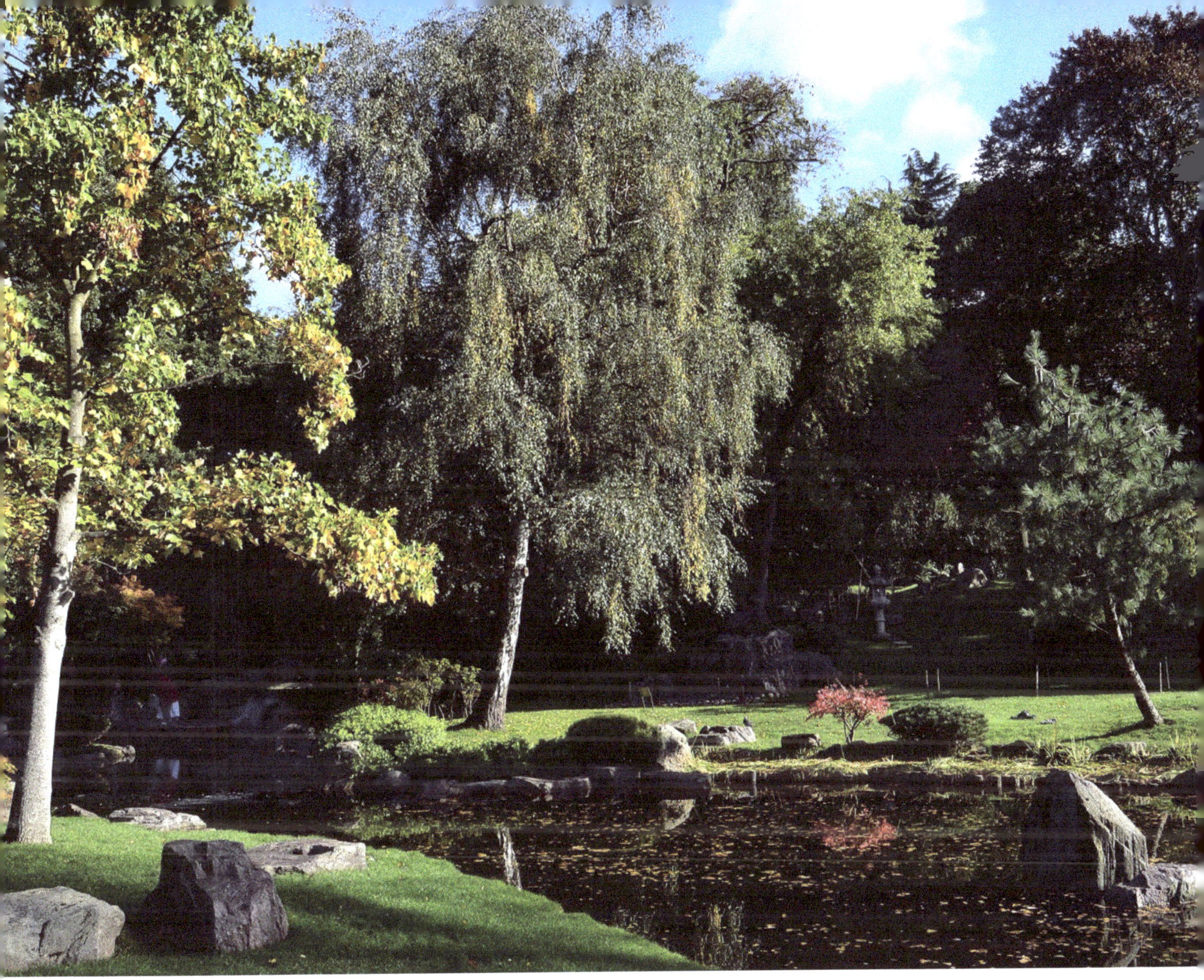

Photo by George Rex

Kyoto Garden

The Kyoto Garden is located inside Holland Park and was donated by the Chamber of Commerce of Kyoto in 1991. It was joined by the Fukushima Memorial Garden in 2012. The park features a wide variety of plants, a trickling waterfall, a rock bridge and even free-roaming peacocks. This is a truly unique sight in one of London's most peaceful parks.

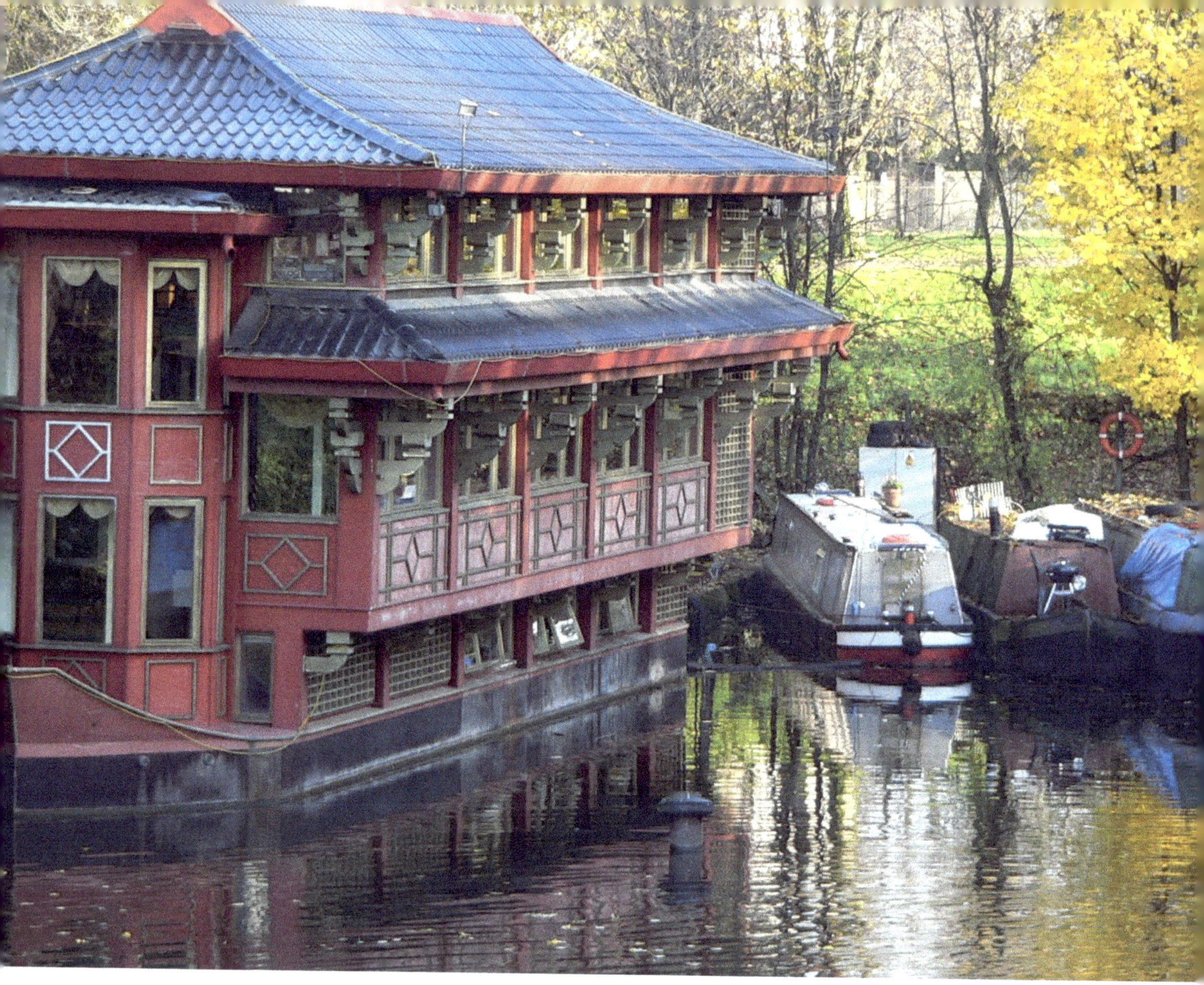

Regent's Park

Photo by S. Pakhrin

Regent's Park was built for the Prince Regent in the 1810s, as a grand setting for a new palace. The palace was never built, but the park survives as a reminder of what could have been. Pictured is Feng Shang Princess, a floating Chinese restaurant located on the Regent's Canal, which runs through the northern part of the park.

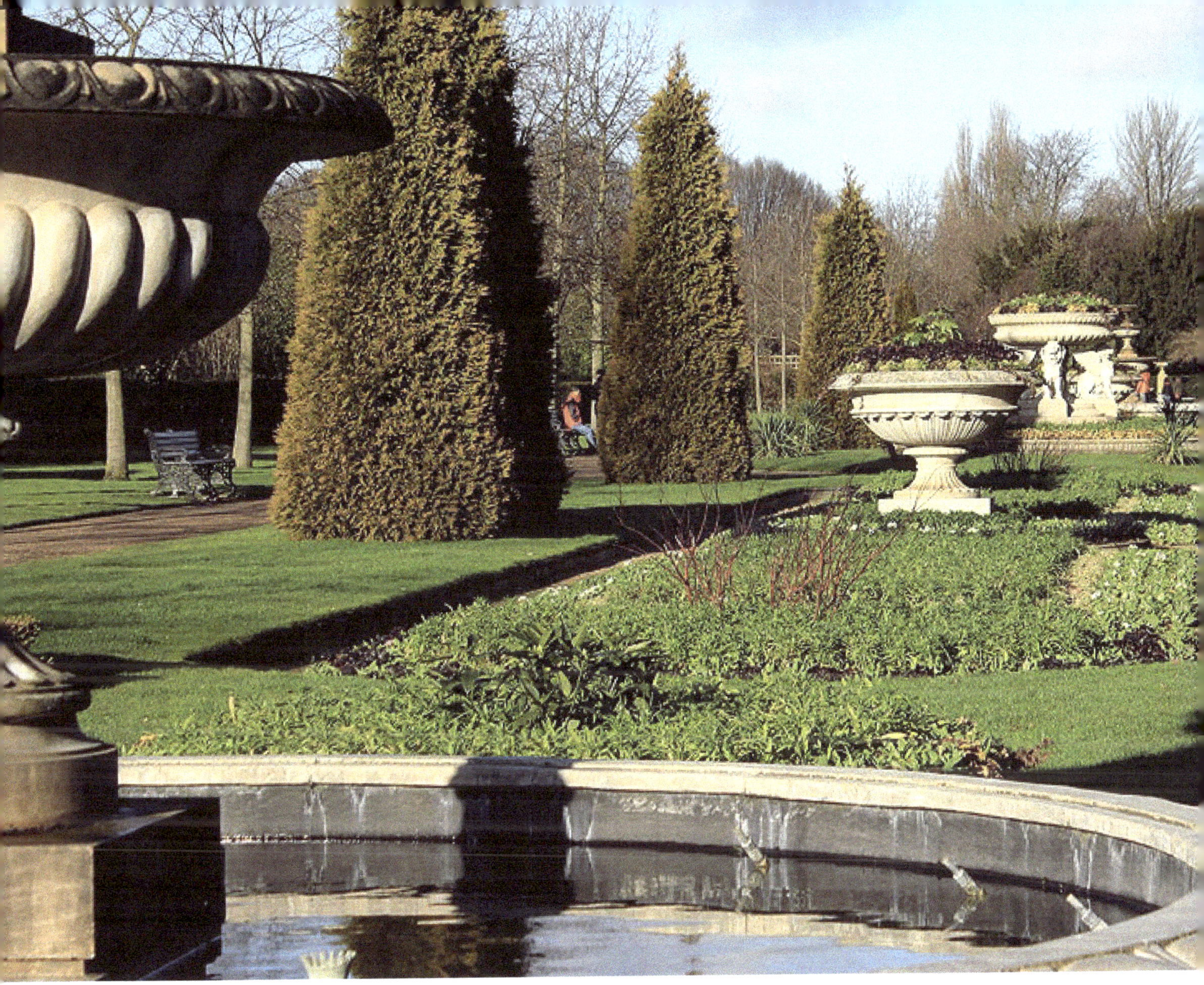

Photo by R. Norton & D. Allen

Regent's Park

Regent's Park opened to the public in 1835 and today houses London Zoo, the world's oldest scientific zoo opened in 1828. Here you can also find Queen Mary's Rose Gardens dating from 1934 with over 12,000 roses, a Japanese garden, an open-air theatre, a boating lake, Regent's University and countless smaller gardens, fountains and memorials.

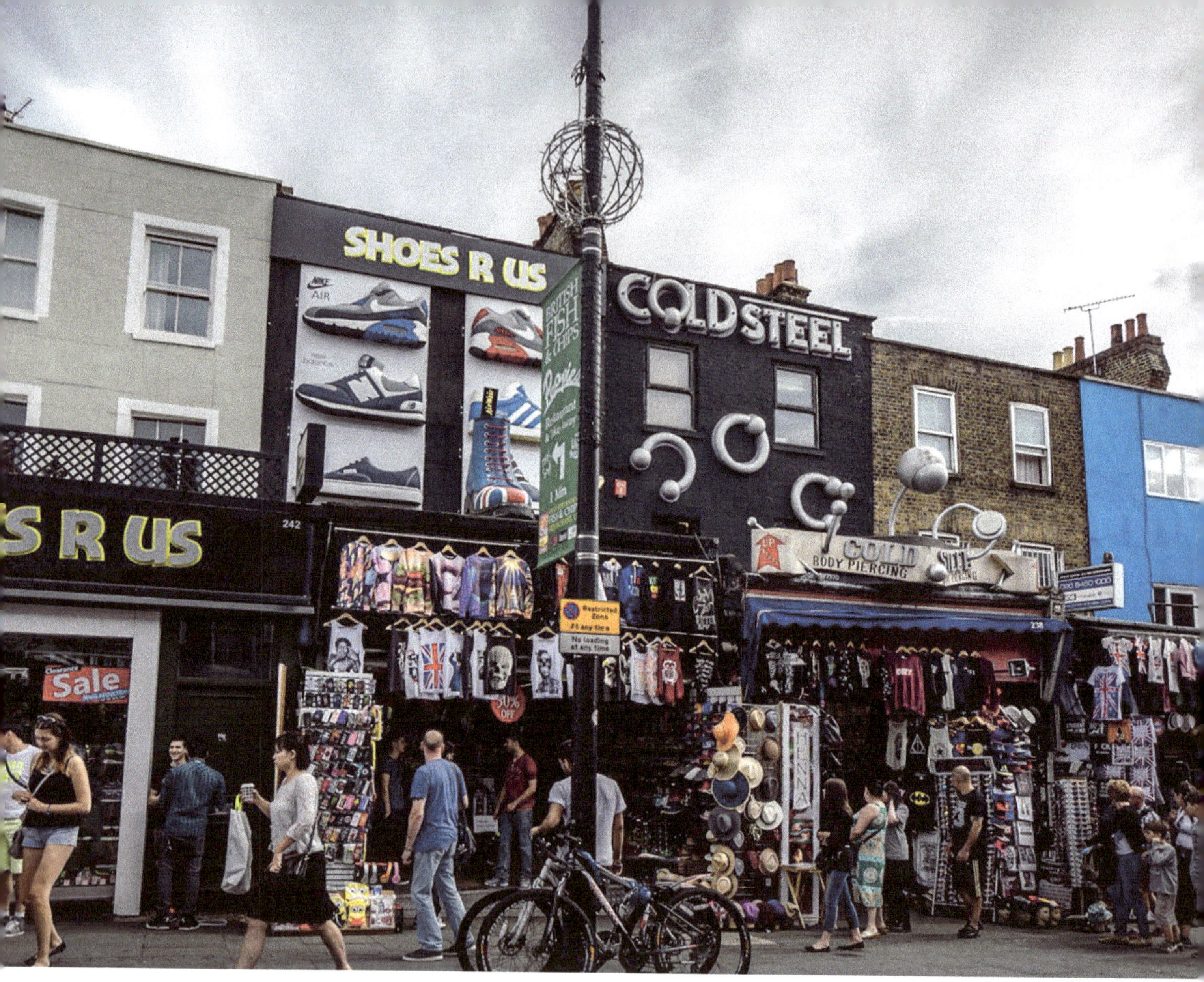

Camden

Photo by Gian Luca Ponti

Camden has been home to London's alternative culture scene since at least the 1970s. Many even say that the 'punk' scene began here. Camden was home to Britain's House scene in the 1980s and Brit Pop in the 1990s. Unfortunately, due to gentrification, the artists that once lived in the area are being pushed out and Camden has changed immensely.

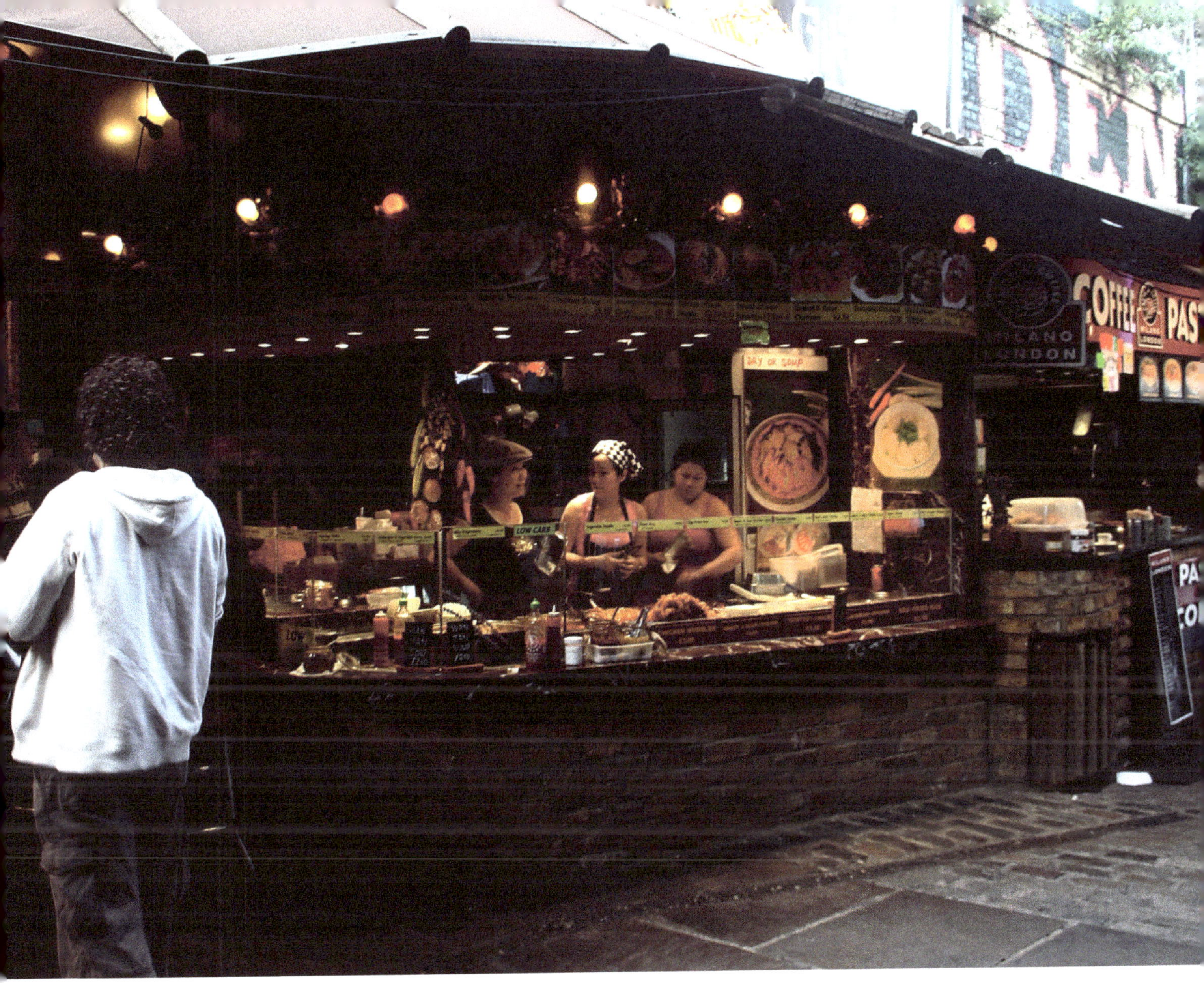

Photo by Phalinn Ooi

Camden Market

Camden Market is, in fact, formed of six individual markets: the two most famous are arguably Camden Lock Market and Stables Market. Inside, you will find handmade goods, second-hand items, antiques and household decorations, as well as a statue to Amy Winehouse who lived nearby at 30 Camden Square.

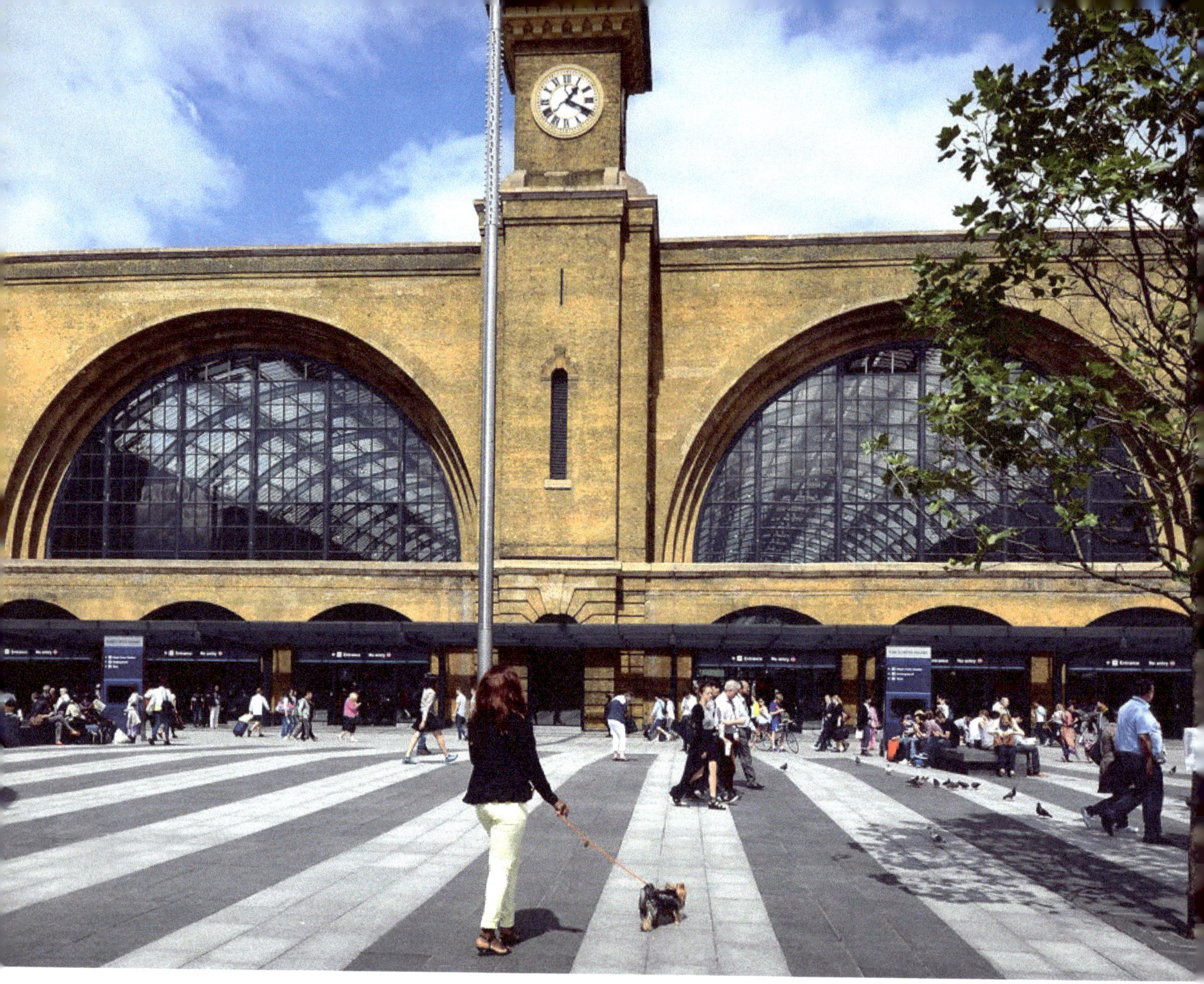

King's Cross

Photo by George Rex

Opened in 1852 by the Great Northern Railway, King's Cross is one of London's grandest stations. The station features heavily in the Harry Potter books and films as the location of Platform 9¾. The station underwent a large transformation between 2007-2012 exposing the station facade (pictured) and removing an extension dating from the 1970s.

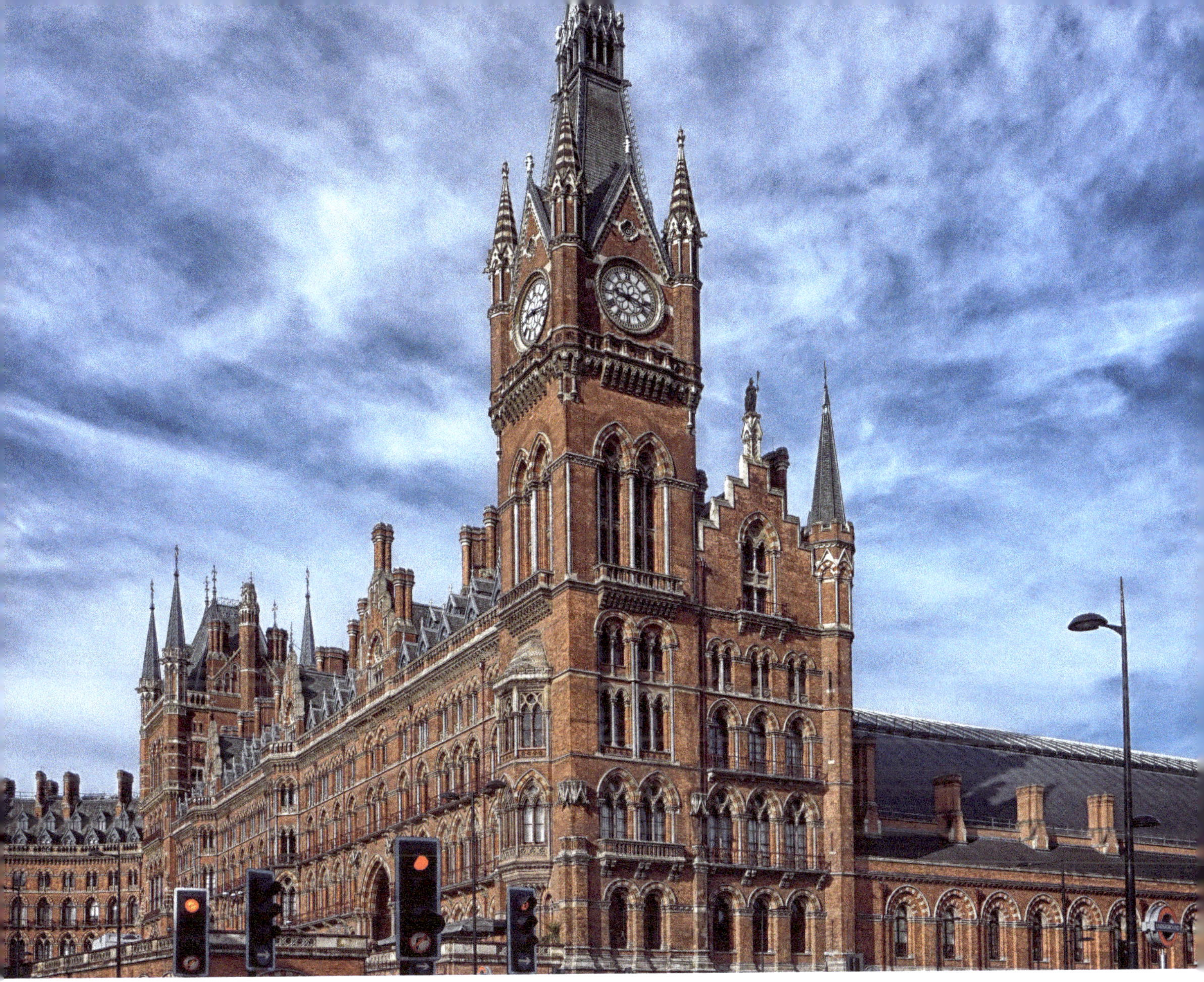

St Pancras Station

Photo by David Skinner

Across the road from King's Cross is St Pancras Station, having opened in 1868. The red-brick facade pictured was opened as the Midland Grand Hotel in 1873; this was then used as railway offices before reopening as a hotel in 2011. St Pancras is the gateway to Paris, Brussels, Amsterdam and other locations via the high-speed Eurostar train service.

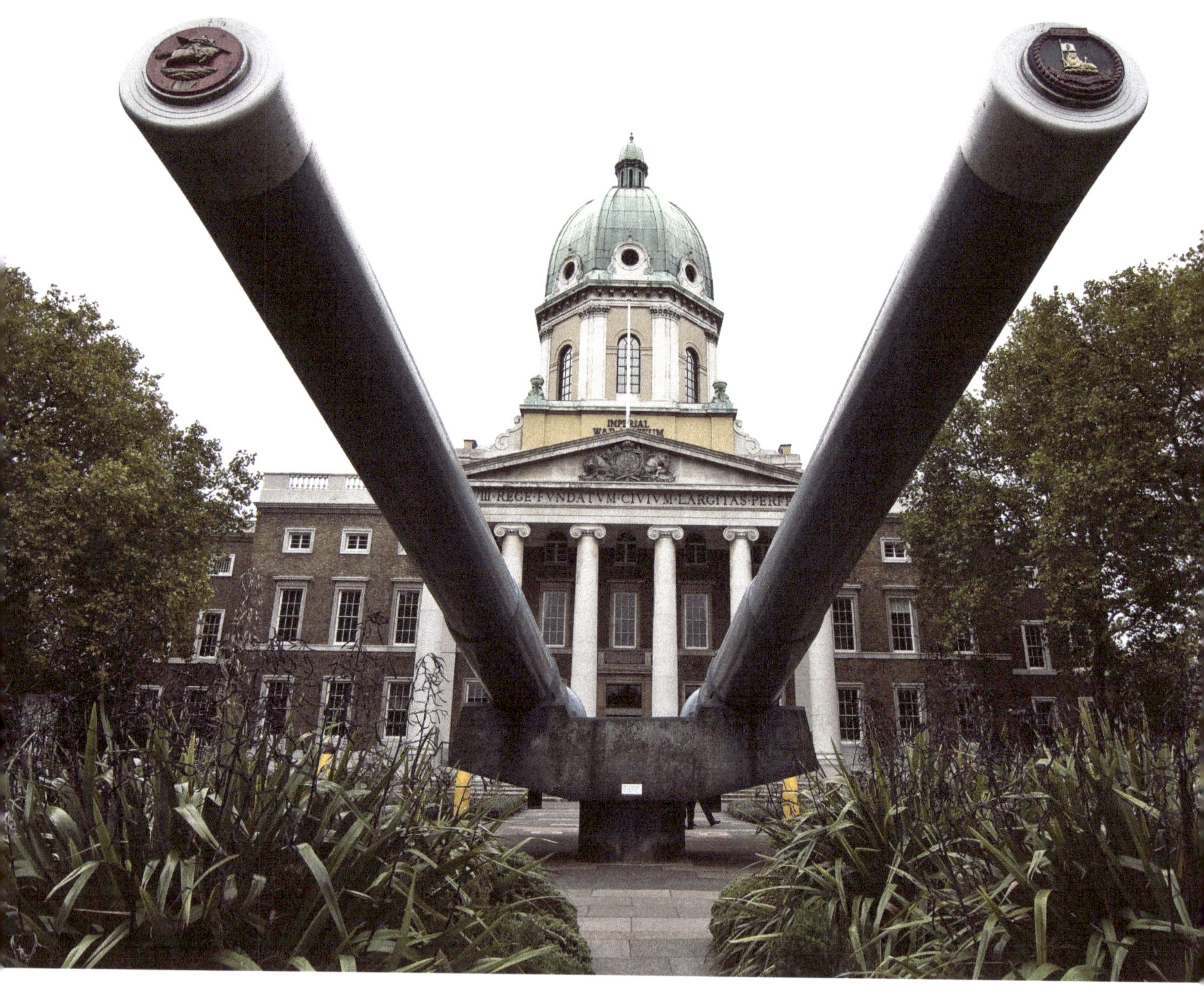

Imperial War Museum

Photo by Jim Bahn

The Imperial War Museum building was a former hospital constructed in 1936. Today the building contains exhibitions over five floors detailing conflicts Britain and other Commonwealth countries have been involved in since 1914. Admission is free and the Imperial War Museum is one of London's most impressive (and lesser known) museums.

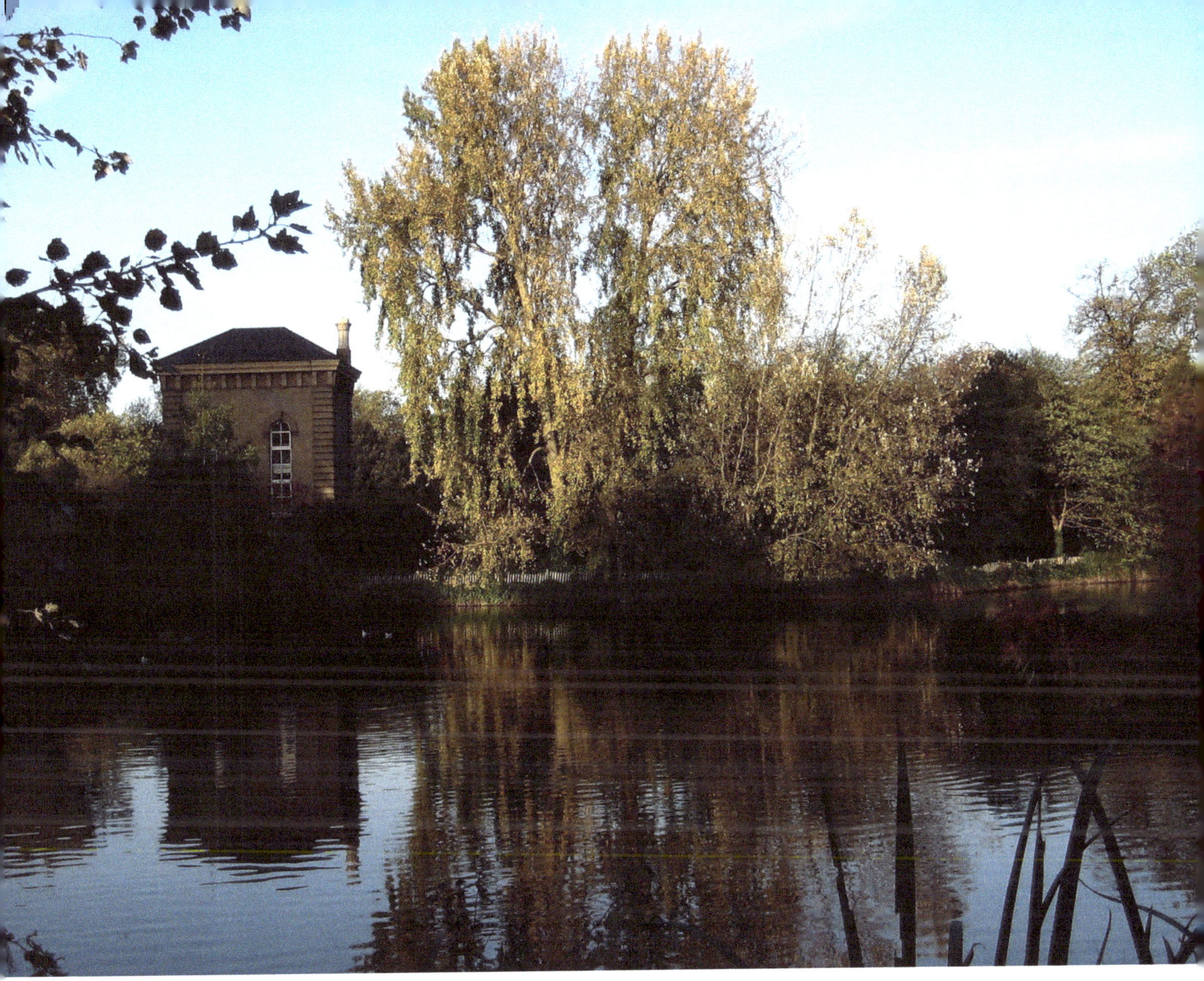

Photo by Georgio

Battersea Park

Spanning 200 acres, Battersea Park is located in south-west London. The park is home to a peace pagoda, a small zoo, a boating lake, a bowling green, several flower gardens, a bike hire shop, and a high ropes course amongst other activities. Pictured across the lake is the Pump House Gallery which showcases contemporary art.

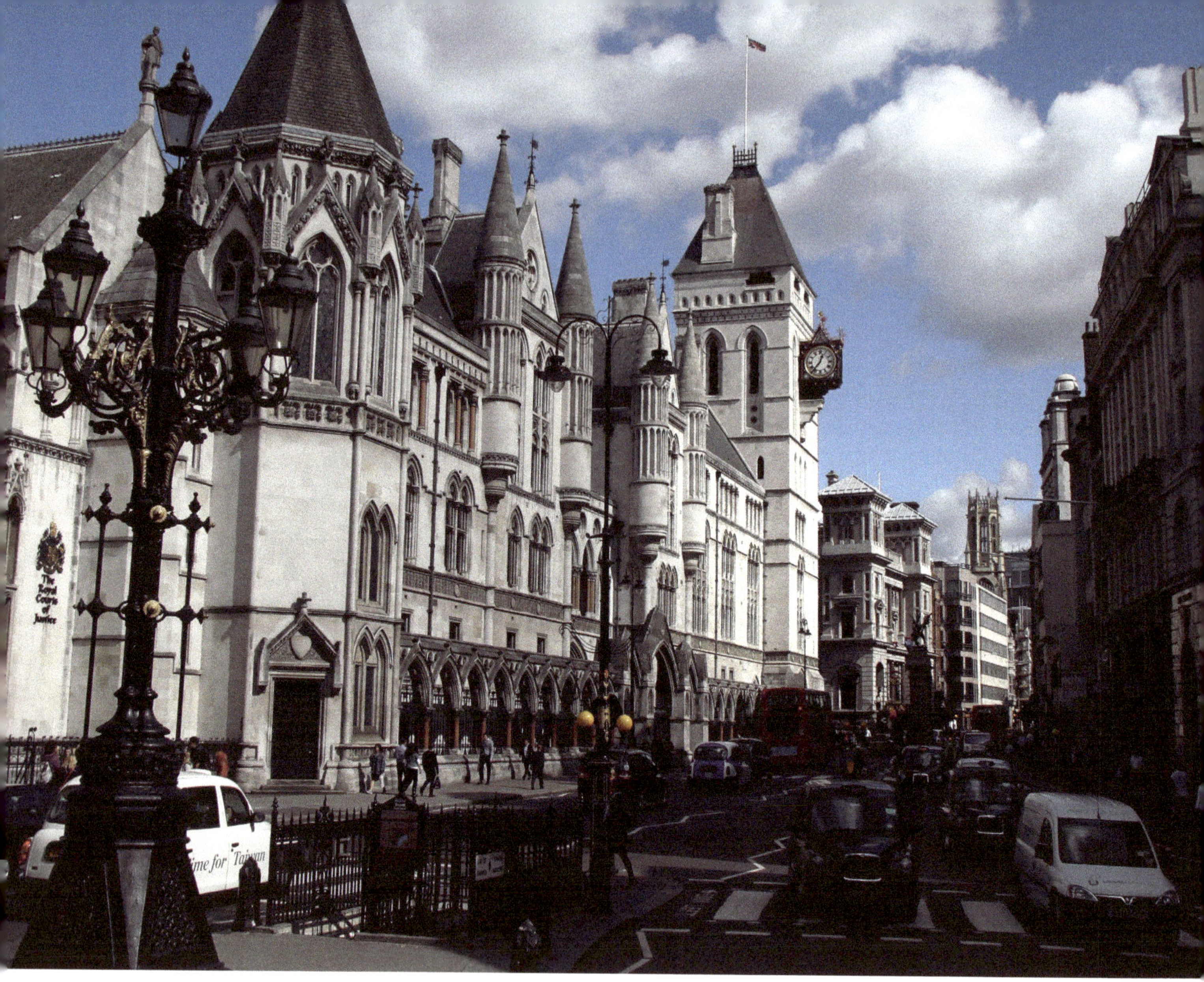

Fleet Street

Photo by Ronnie Macdonald

Fleet Street is synonymous in the UK with the newspaper industry and was once known as "the street of ink". Indeed, the first daily newspaper in Britain - the Daily Courant - was published here in 1702. Number 186 Fleet Street is home to fictional character Sweeney Todd, a murderering barber, immortalised in the story The String of Pearls.

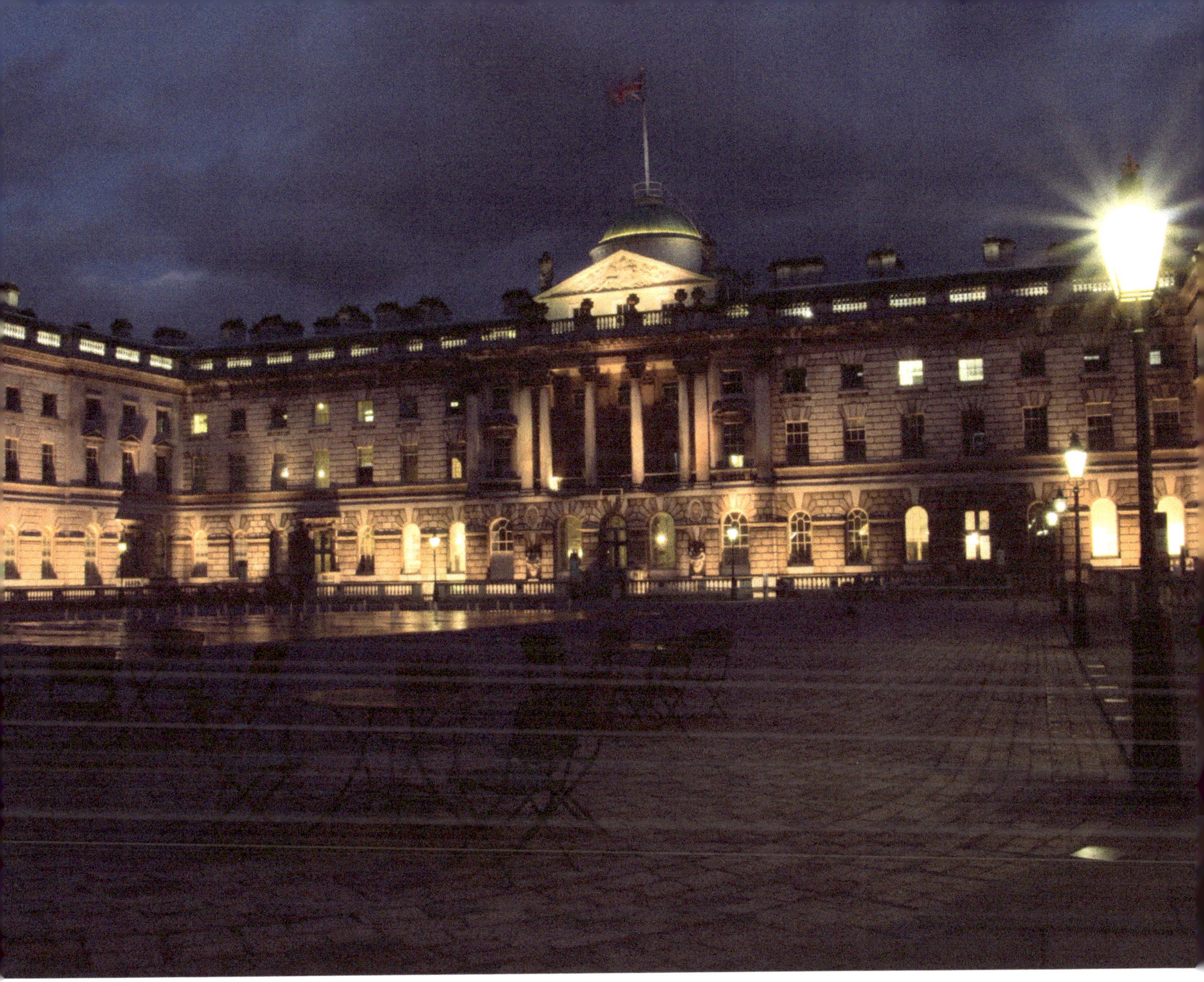

Photo by Kenneth Fleming

Somerset House

Designed by William Chambers, this 18th century building was built as government offices. Today it is mainly used for events such as London Fashion Week. It is also the home of the Courtauld Gallery - mostly French Impressionist paintings - and other galleries. It was originally the site of a riverside house owned by Edward Seymour (Duke of Somerset).

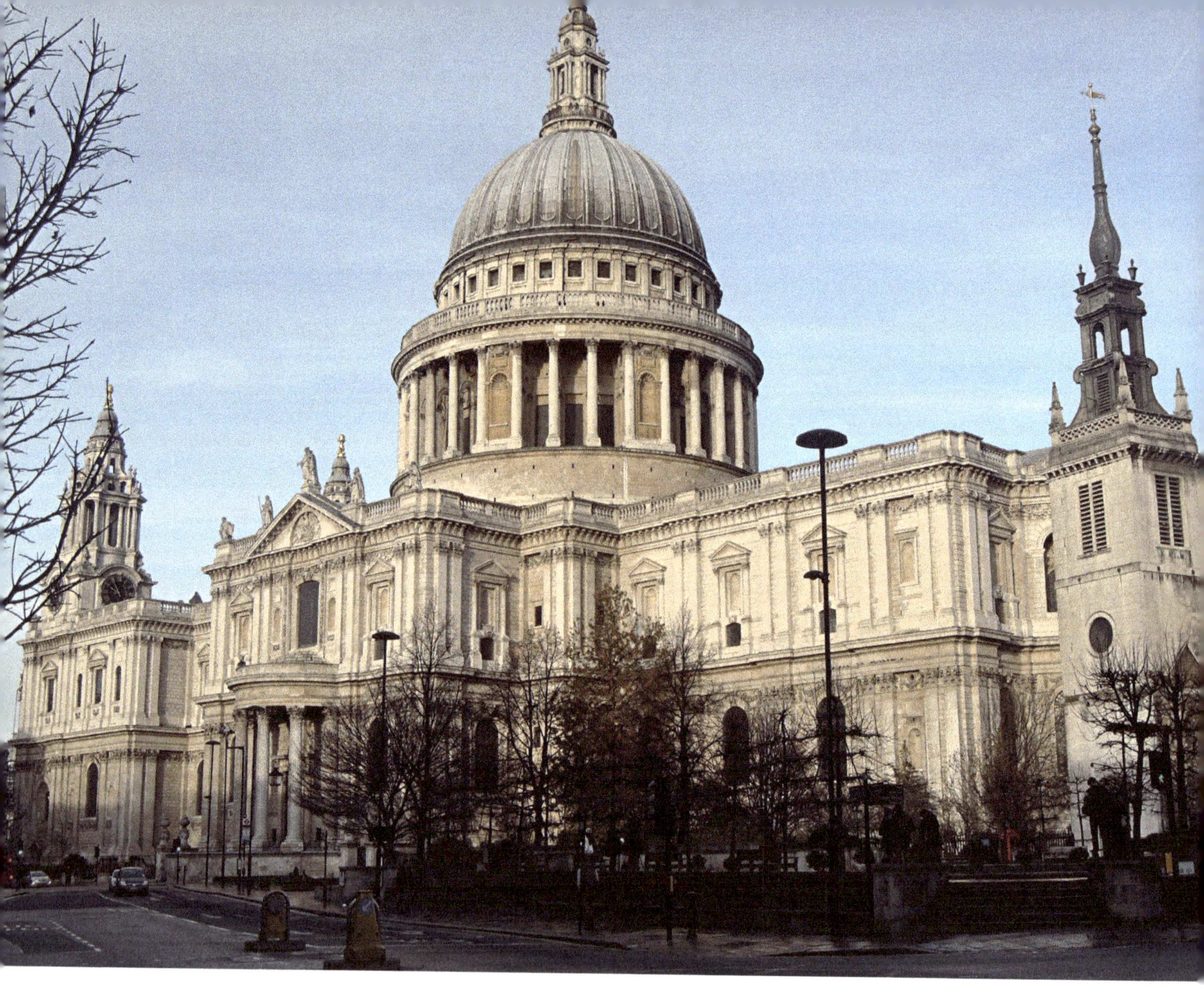

St Paul's Cathedral

Photo by Loco Steve

The origins of the first church on this site dedicated to Paul the Apostle date back to AD 604. Today's Cathedral building was designed by Sir Christopher Wren and replaced a church destroyed in The Great Fire of London. The church was completed in 1710 and remained the tallest building in London until 1967. This is the largest church in London.

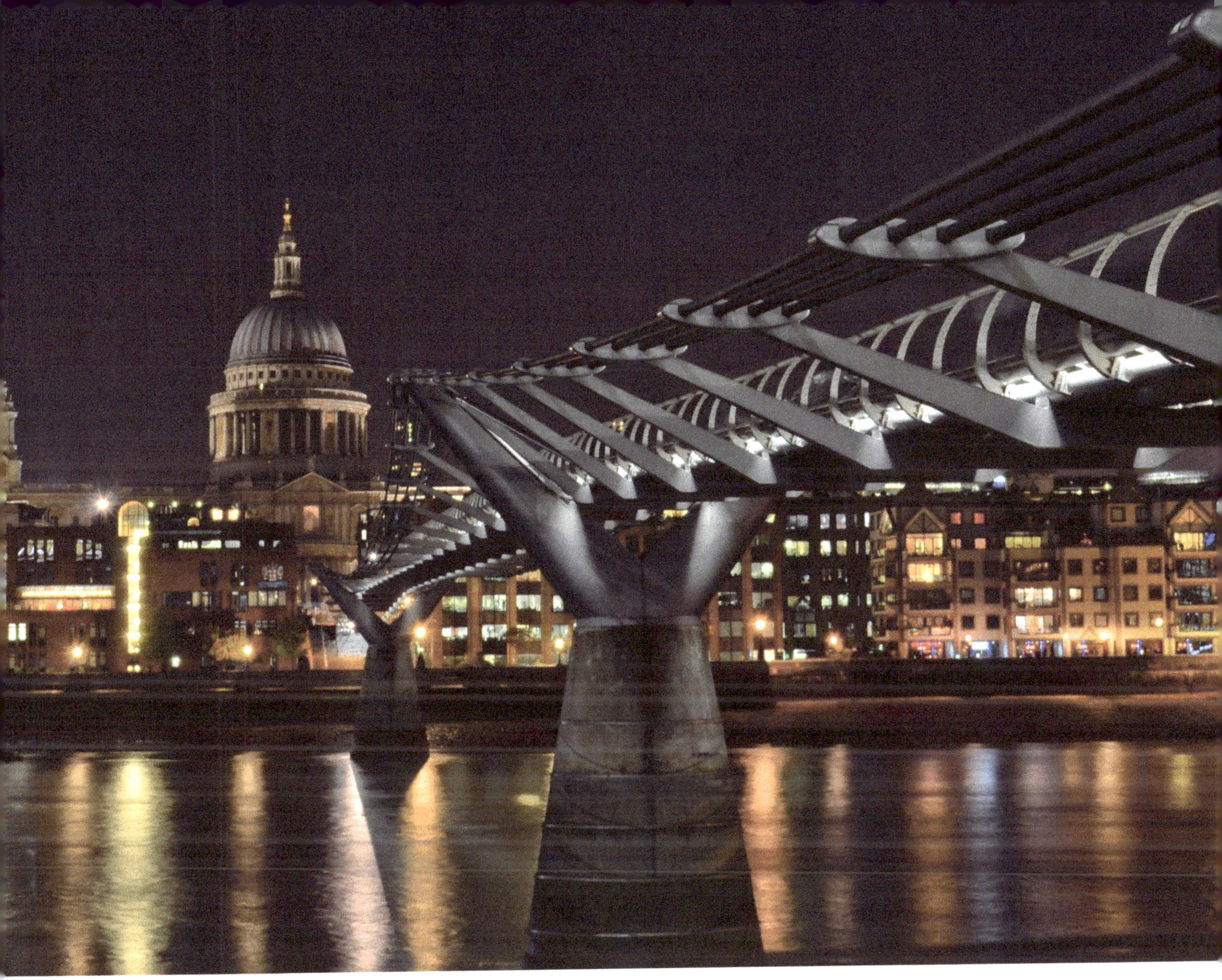

Millennium Bridge

Photo by Garry Knight

The Millennium Bridge (opened in 2000) is also known as the "Wobbly Bridge" due to an engineering oversight when it was first unveiled which caused the bridge to sway from side to side in an effect known as "synchronous lateral excitation". The bridge re-opened two years later after being fixed. It was designed by Foster and Partners.

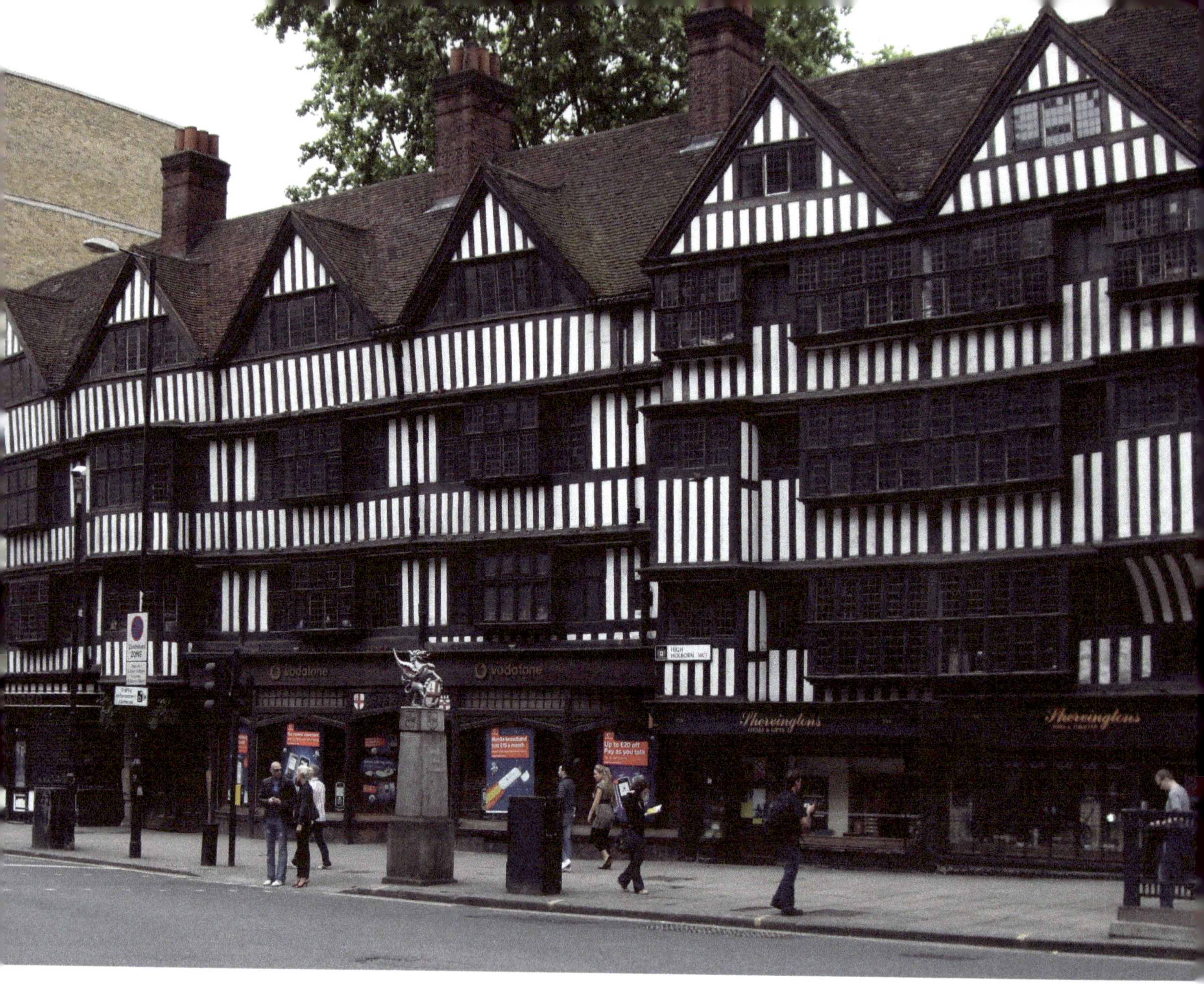

Staple Inn

Photo by Jim Linwood

Staple Inn was built in 1585 as a wool staple, where wool was weighed and taxed. It was also part of Gray's Inn, a professional association for barristers (lawyers). The building is one of the few that survived the 1666 Great Fire of London. It was restored in the 20th century and today is used as for meetings by The Institute and Faculty of Actuaries.

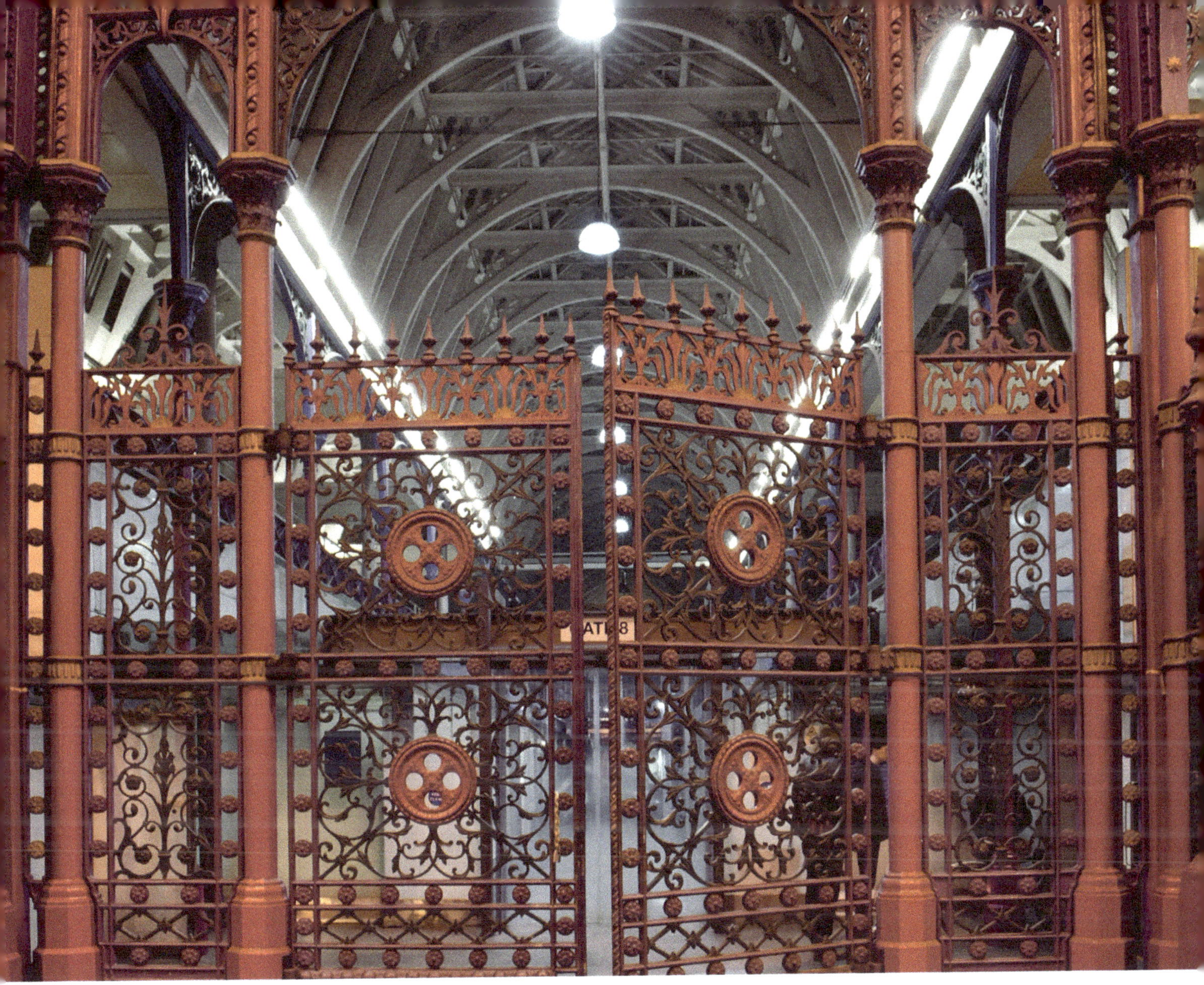

Smithfield Market

Photo by Garry Knight

The first market on this site dates from the 10th century when it handled livestock. By the 19th century, the market had transitioned to selling meat and fish for hygiene reasons. The current market buildings with their cast iron details were designed by Sir Horace Jones and completed in 1868. Smithfield Market is still used as a wholesale meat market today.

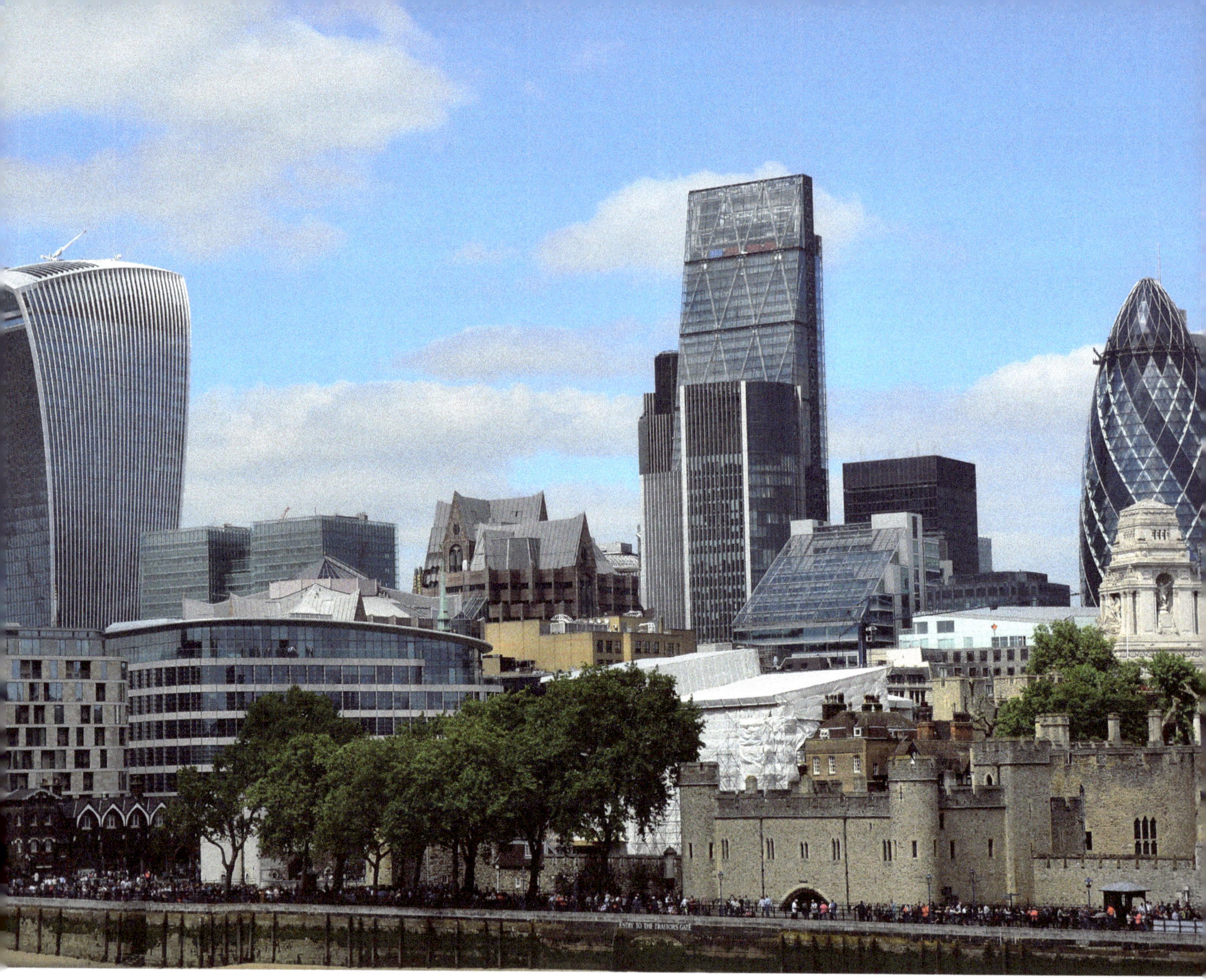

City of London

Photo by Martin Pettitt

The City of London was the area where the Romans settled in London in the 1st century, and spans just over 1 square mile. It is distinct from Greater London. Today, The City of London is the world's premier financial district with over 300,000 people working in this small area and over 45% of the world's foreign currency exchange taking place here.

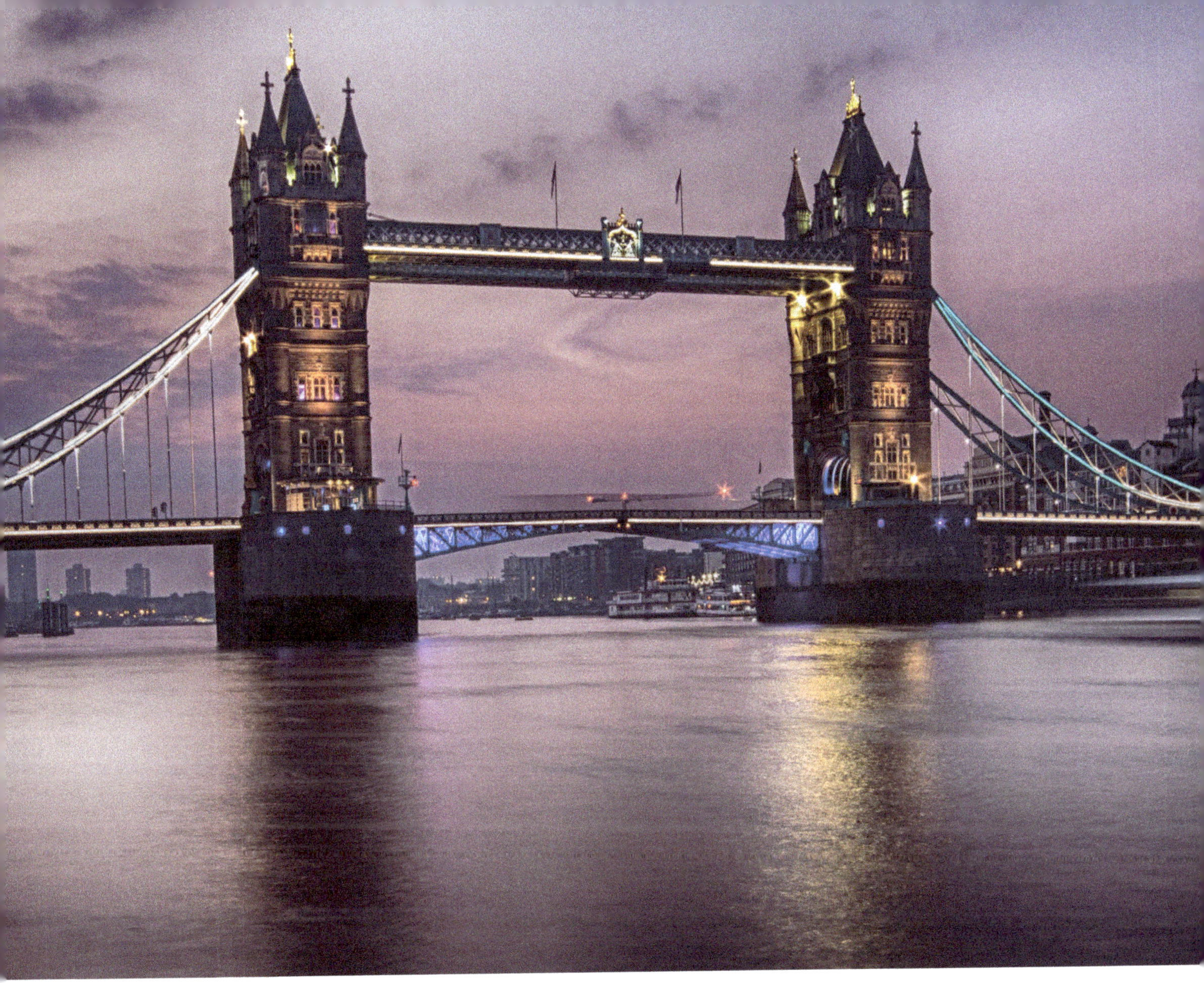

Photo by UlyssesThirtyOne

Tower Bridge

Designed by Sir Horace Jones, Tower Bridge was constructed to ease congestion on the nearby London Bridge. The bridge features bascules or drawbridges which raise to allow tall ships to pass through. The frame of the bridge is made of steel and stone cladding is used on the towers to give the bridge an older appearance - it opened in 1894.

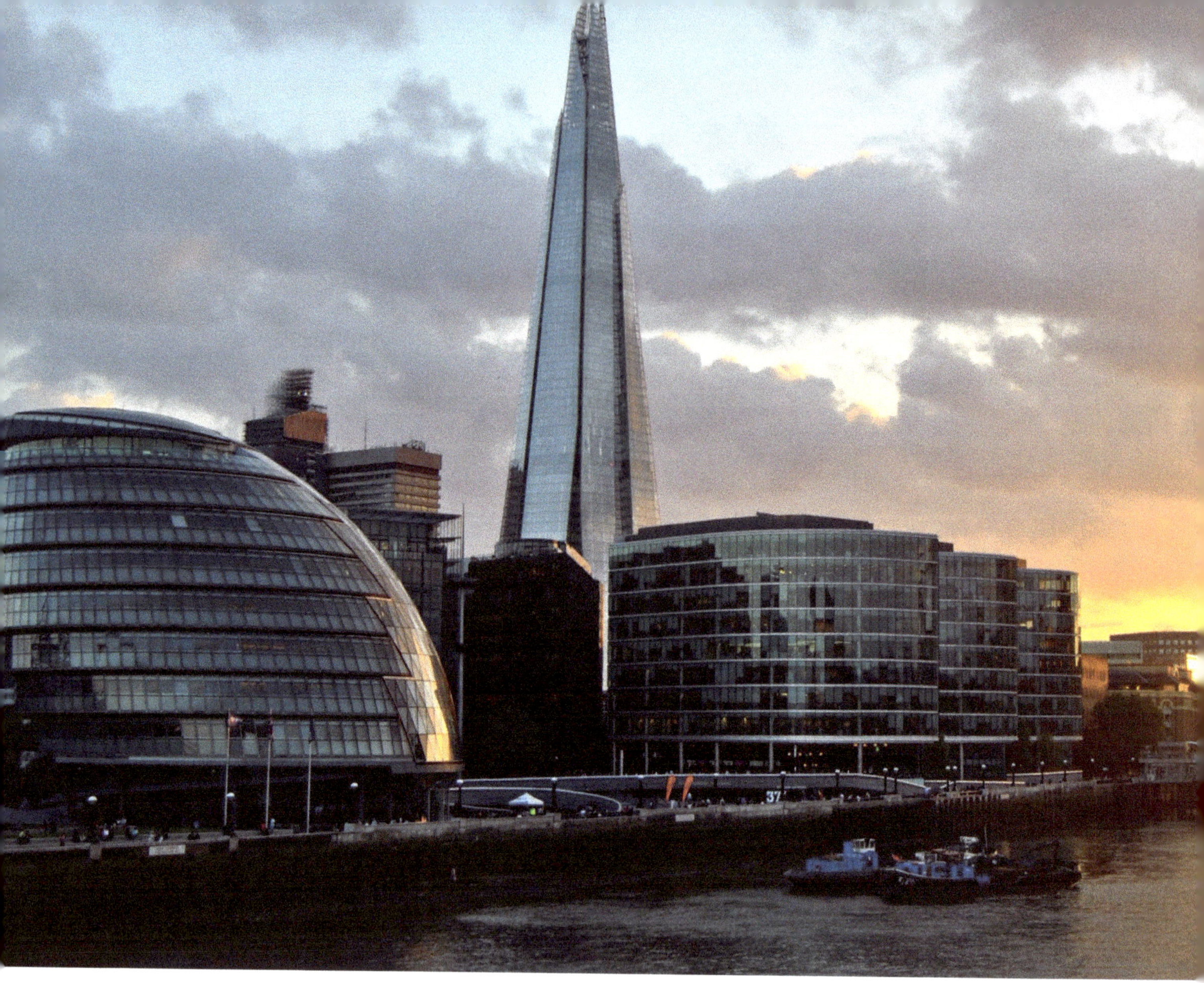

City Hall & The Shard

Photo by Loco Steve

City Hall is home to the Greater London Council and is the office of the Mayor of London; it was unveiled in 2002 and has become the centrepiece for the redevelopment of the local area called "More London". The tallest building in the photograph is The Shard which was completed in 2012. The Shard stands 1,016ft tall and was designed by Renzo Piano.

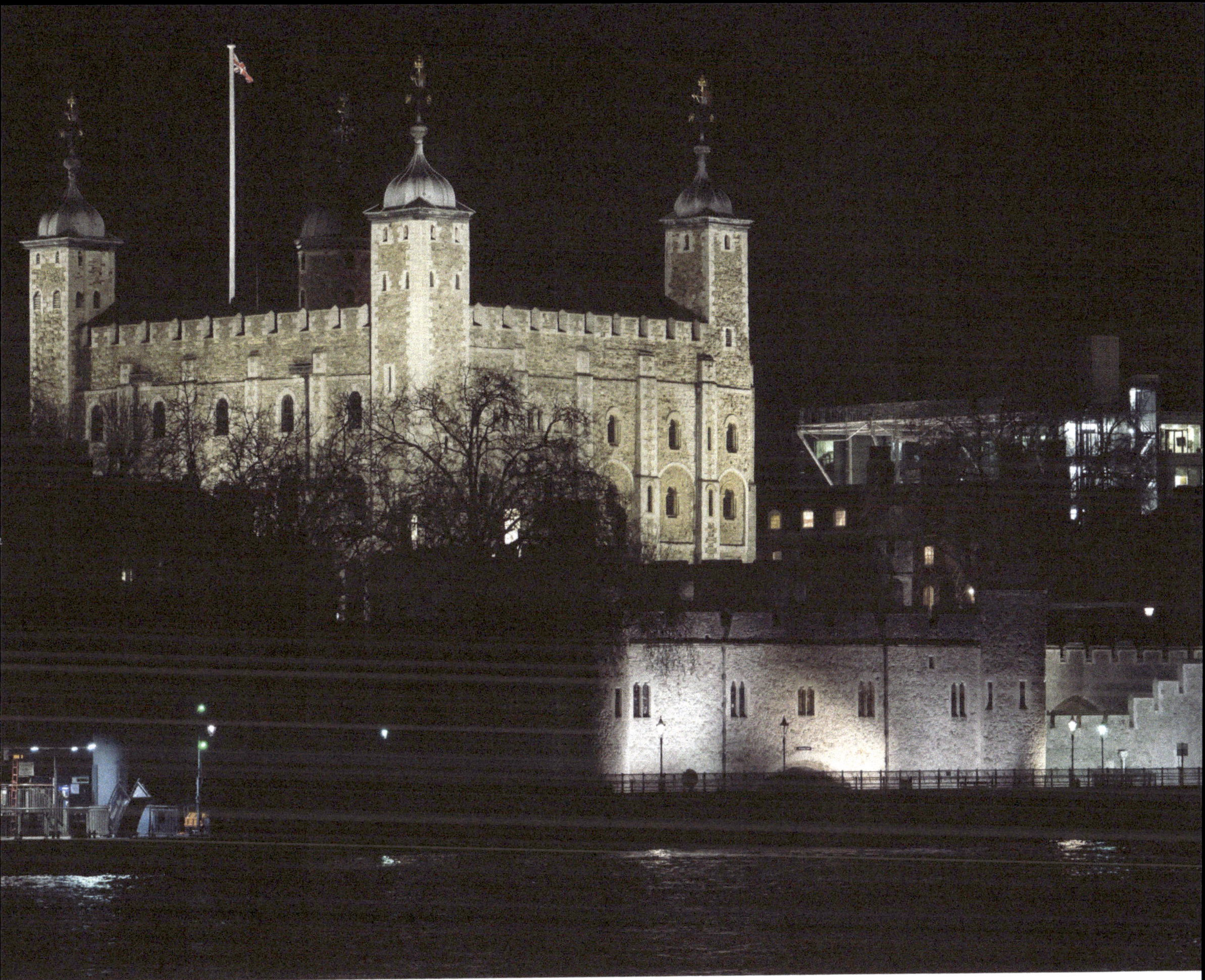

Tower of London

Photo by James E. Petts

The earliest parts of the Tower of London date from 1078, when it was built for William I. It has been home to many monarchs over the years include notably King Henry VIII who had two of his wives beheaded here. Today the Crown Jewels of the United Kingdom are stored at The Tower and are visible to the public, as is a large part of the castle.

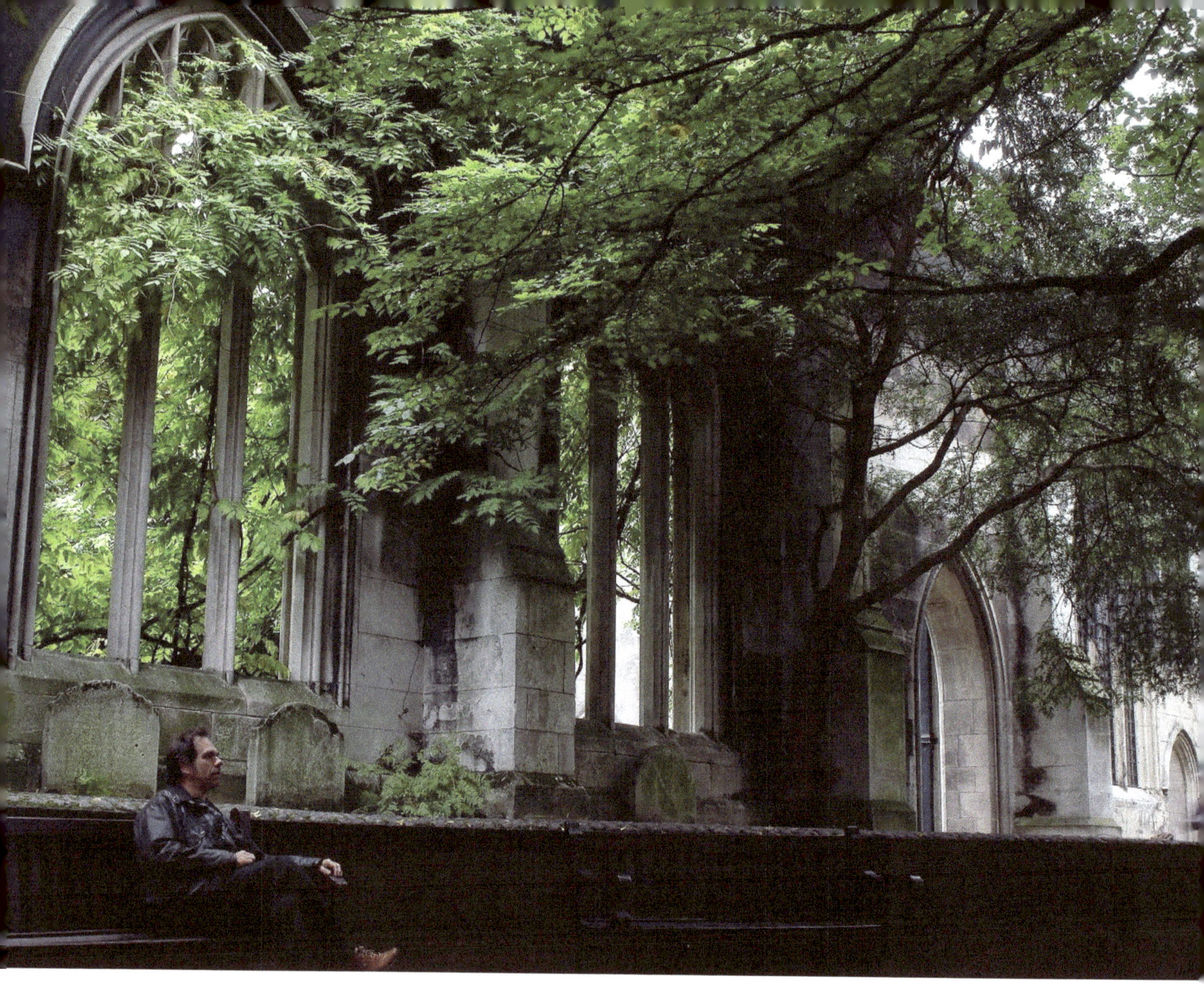

St Dunstan-in-the-East

Photo by Peter G Trimming

The first St Dunstan was built on this site in the 12th century. The church was severely damaged in the Great Fire of London in 1666; it was repaired and architect Sir Christopher Wren added a new steeple in a Gothic style. The Blitz air raids in WWII severely damaged the church - instead of rebuilding the church yet again, this is now a public garden.

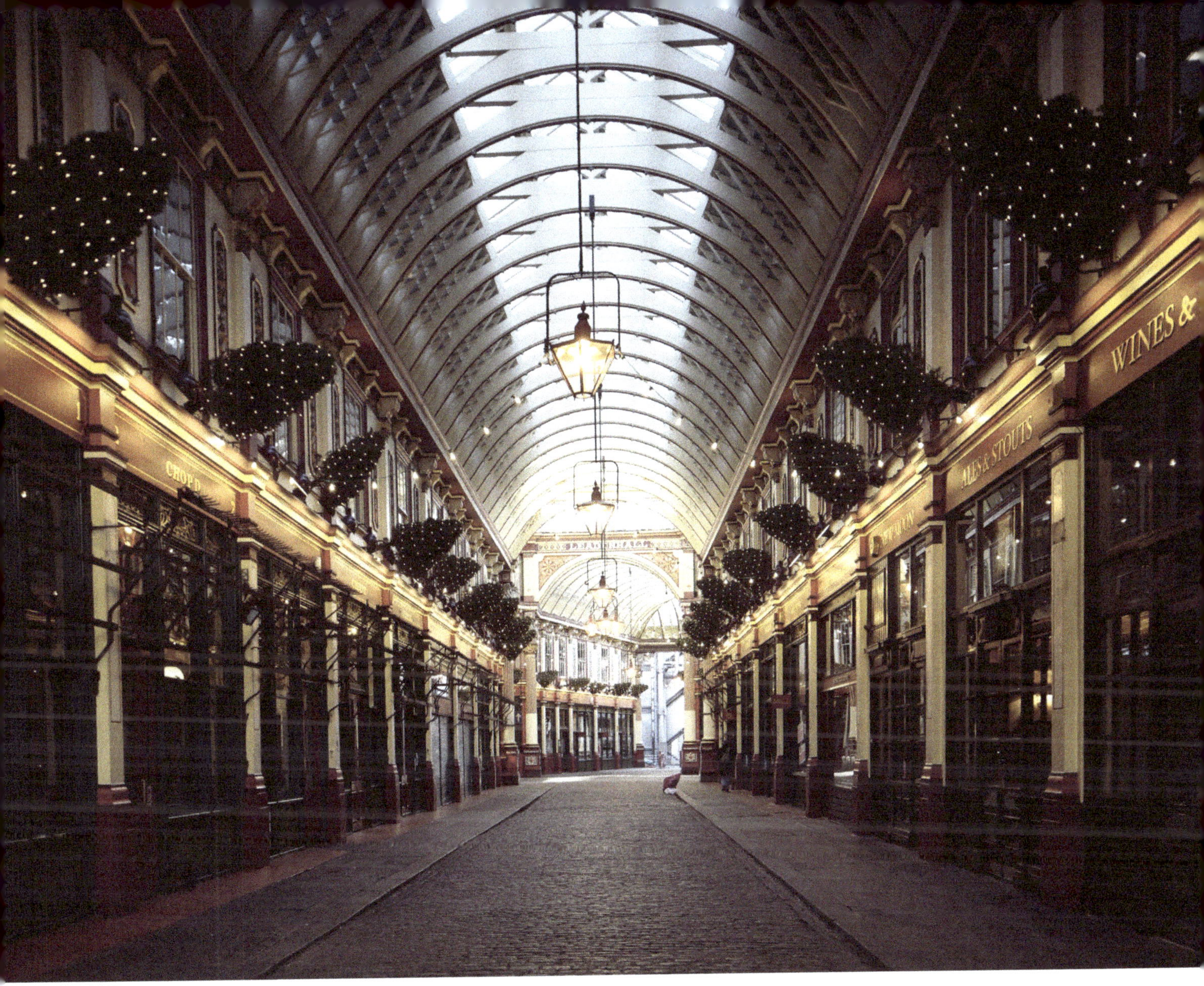

Leadenhall Market

Photo by Aurelien Guichard

Leadenhall Market dates back to 1321, when it was originally a meat market. The current design of the market roof is Victorian, designed in 1881 by Sir Horace Jones who also designed Tower Bridge and other markets in The City. Leadenhall Market was used in the first Harry Potter film as one of the exterior locations for Diagon Alley.

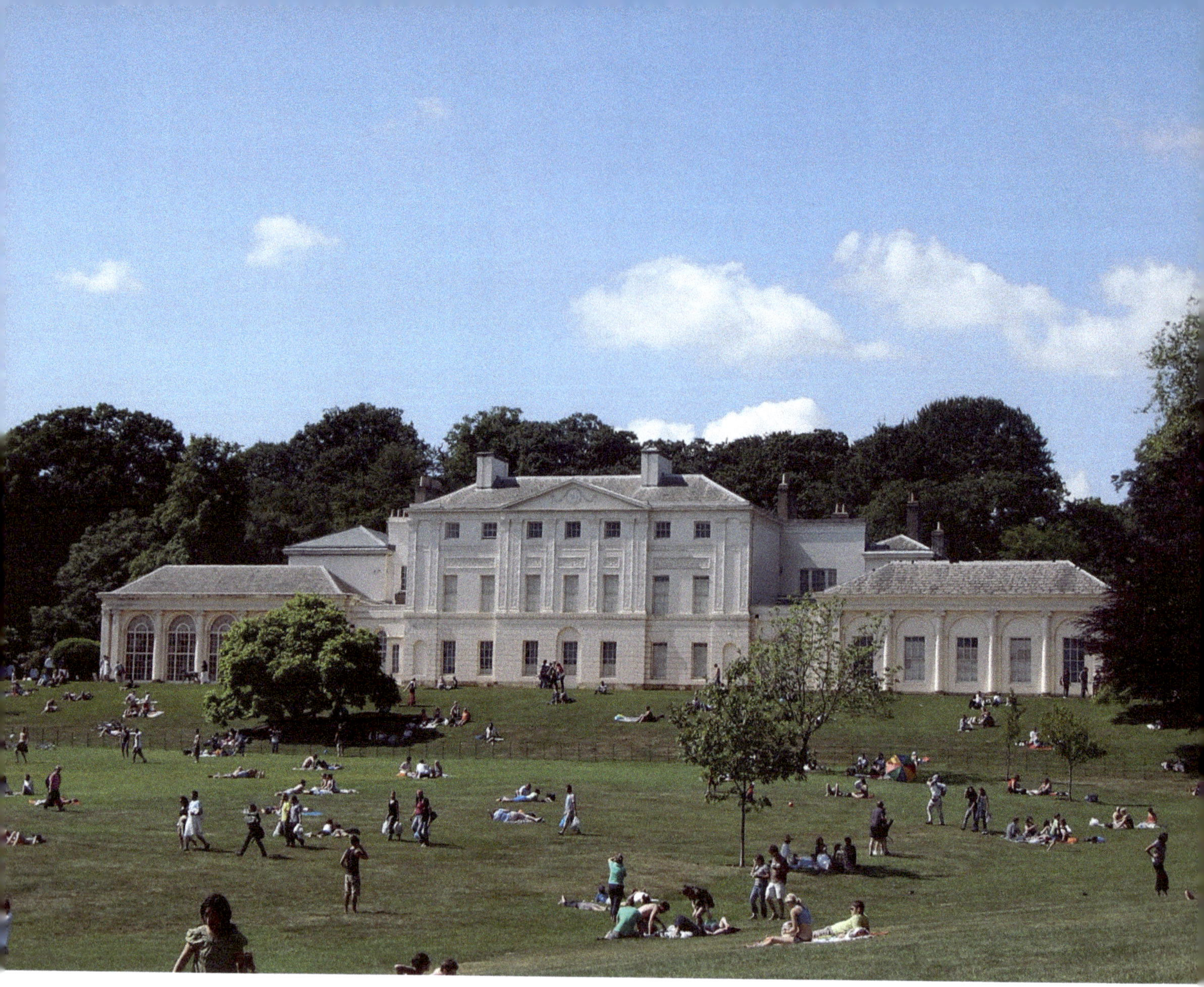

Kenwood House

Photo by Magnus D

Kenwood House dates from the 17th century when it was built as the seat for aristocracy. Over the years it has been used by both the Murray and Guinness families. Today the building is managed by English Heritage, and Kenwood House is accessible to the public at no charge. Kenwood House is located in Hampstead Heath in north London.

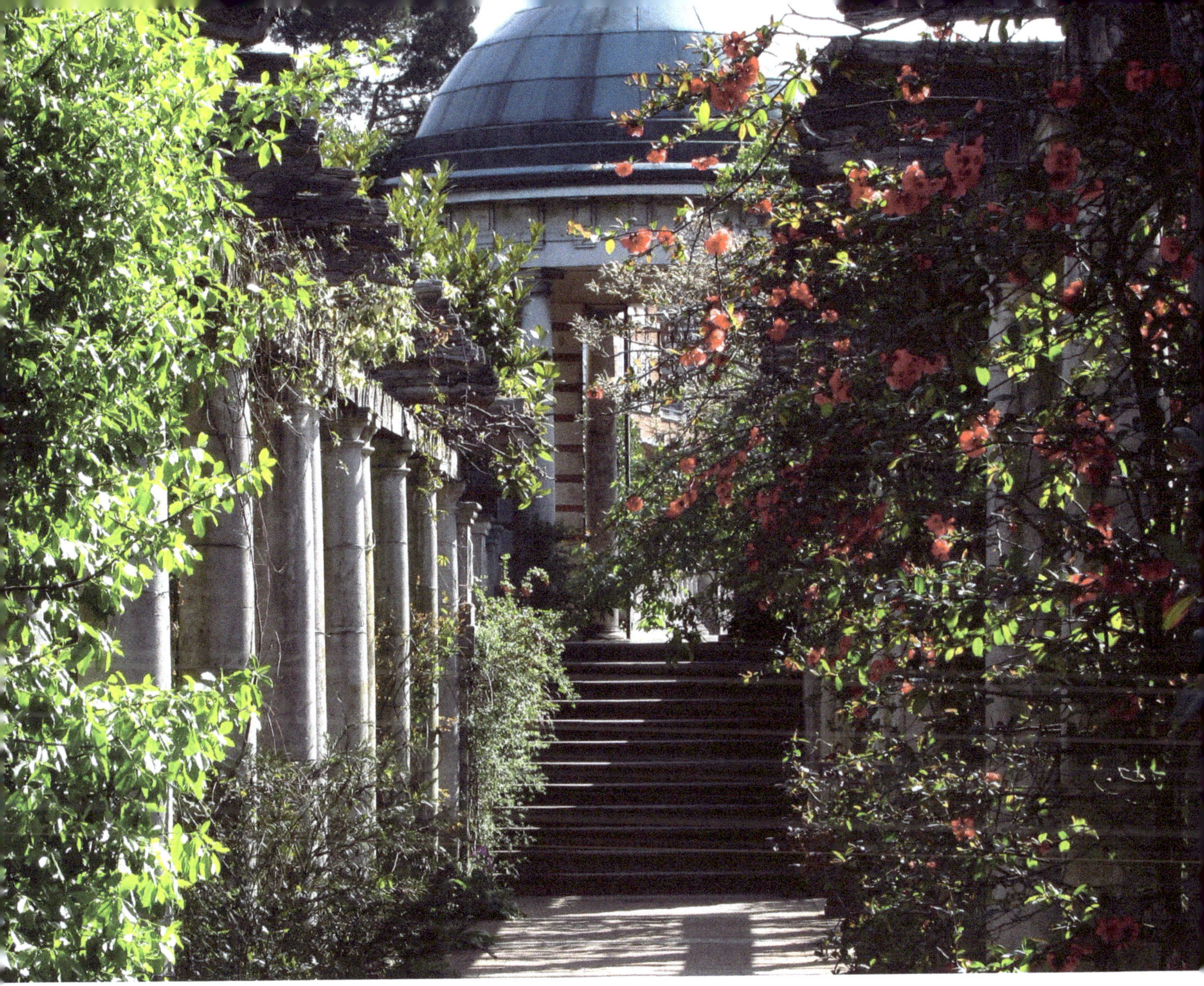

Photo by Laura Nolte

Hampstead Pergola

Hampstead Pergola and gardens were created for Lord Leverhulme in 1905. They were designed by Thomas Mawson as a location for entertaining guests and as a private garden to an enormous house called The Hill. After a period of disrepair, the gardens were restored in the 1990s to their former glory and the area is now open to the public at no charge.

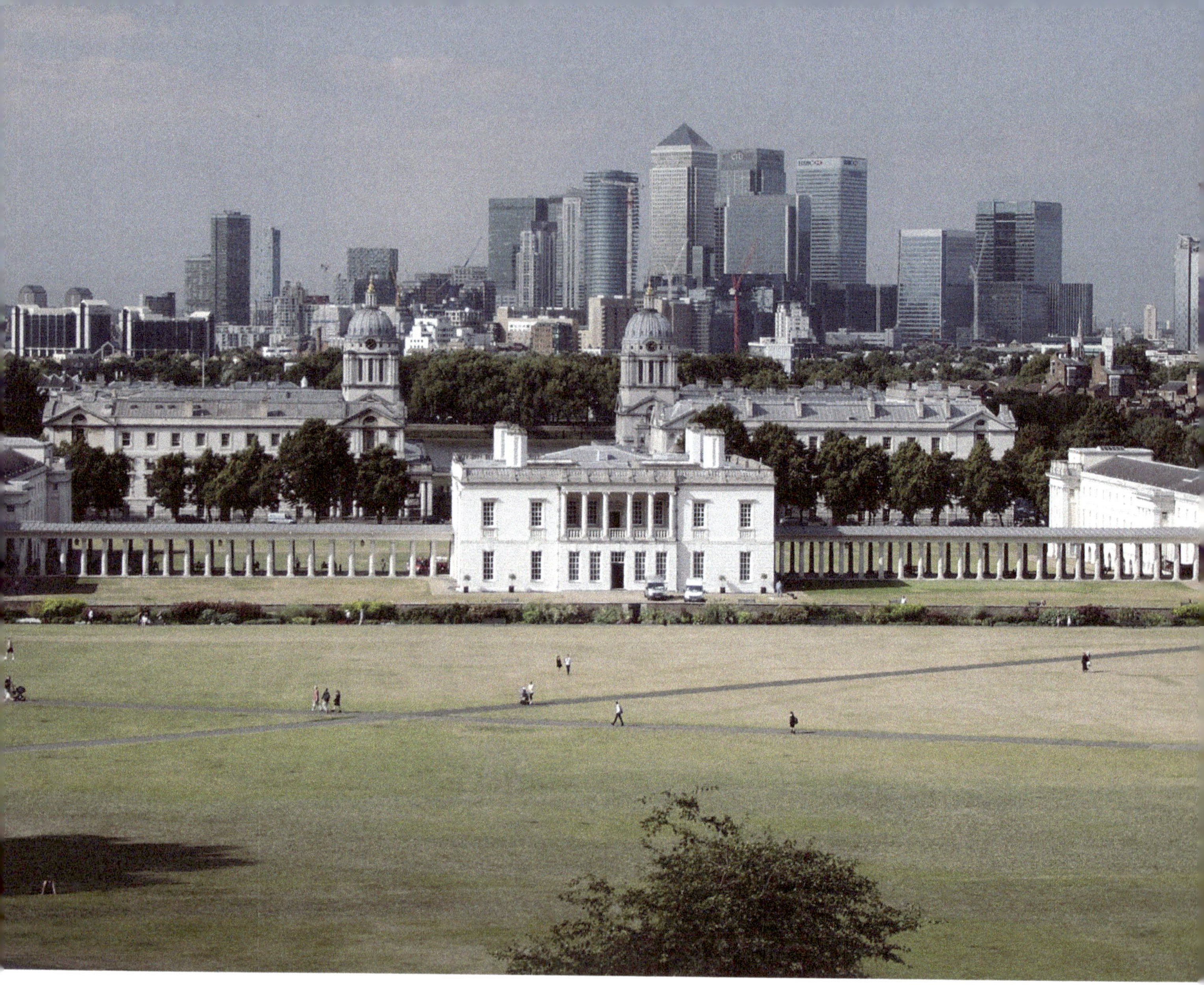

Greenwich

Photo by Leo S

Greenwich is a World Heritage Site located in south east London and is home to the Greenwich Meridian. The area has a strong naval history; the white buildings pictured were formerly the Royal Naval Hospital, later the Royal Naval College, and today are the University of Greenwich. In the distance are Canary Wharf's skyscrapers.

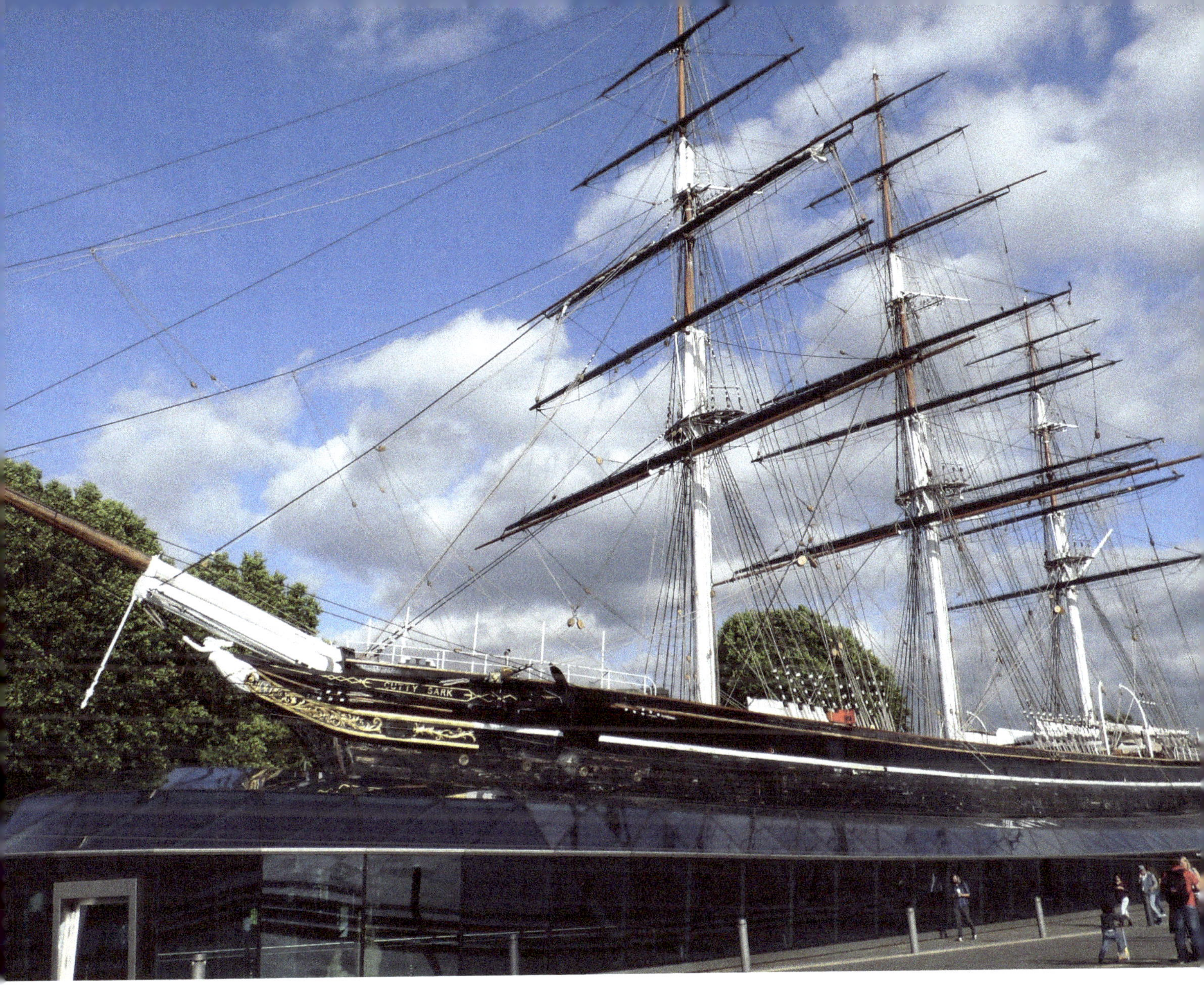

Photo by Szymon Sieciński

Cutty Sark

The Cutty Sark, dating from 1869, was one of the last tea clippers ever built, and also one of the fastest. The ship was used in the tea trade from India, as well as for transporting wool from Australia. The ship was renamed Ferreira by a Portuguese company and was a cargo ship until 1922. It suffered a major fire in 2007 and was painstakingly restored.

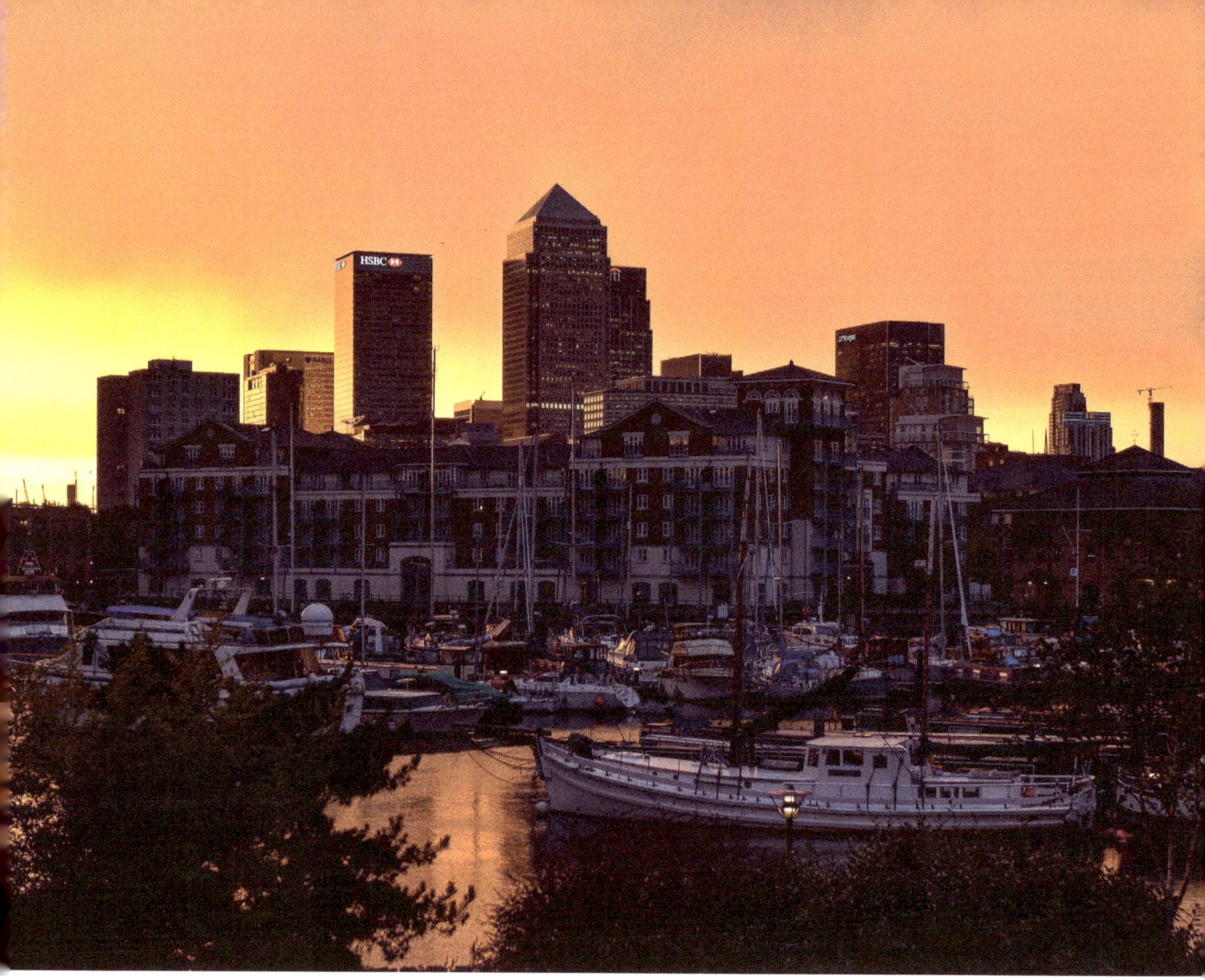

Limehouse Marina

Photo by Winniepix

The Limehouse Basin Marina is the link between the serene Regent's Canal and the tidal River Thames. It is located approximately 1.7 miles east of Tower Bridge. Today the basin is surrounded by expensive homes, but in the 19th century this was a bustling location where coal was transported onto canal boats to reach the gasworks along the canal.

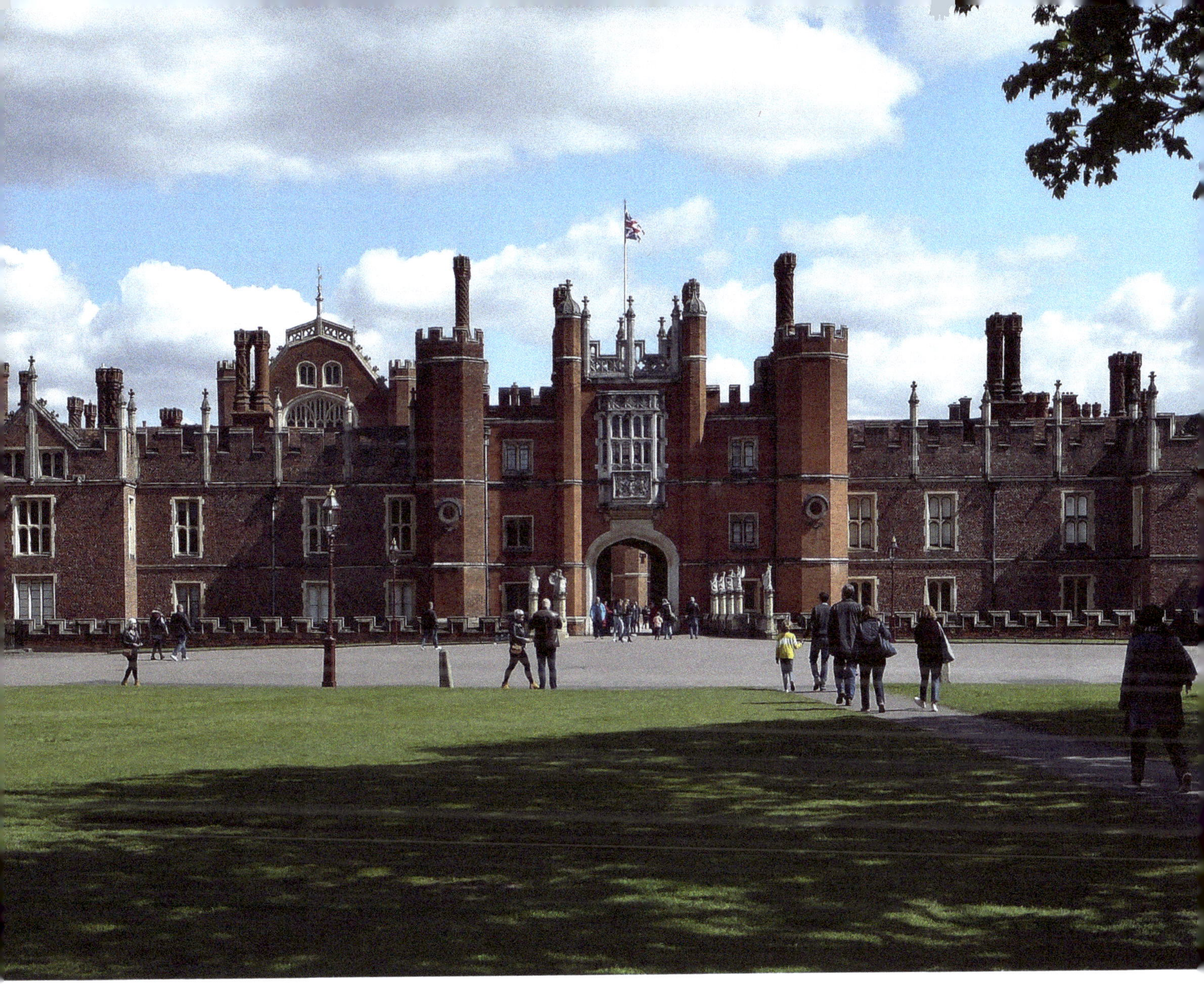

Hampton Court Palace

Photo by Roman Hobler

Hampton Court Palace is located in south west London and was built for Cardinal Thomas Wolsey in 1515. It was later seized by King Henry VIII. William III expanded the palace in the late 17th century so that it could rival Versailles in France, leading to the palace being a mix of different architectural styles. The palace is open to the public for a charge.

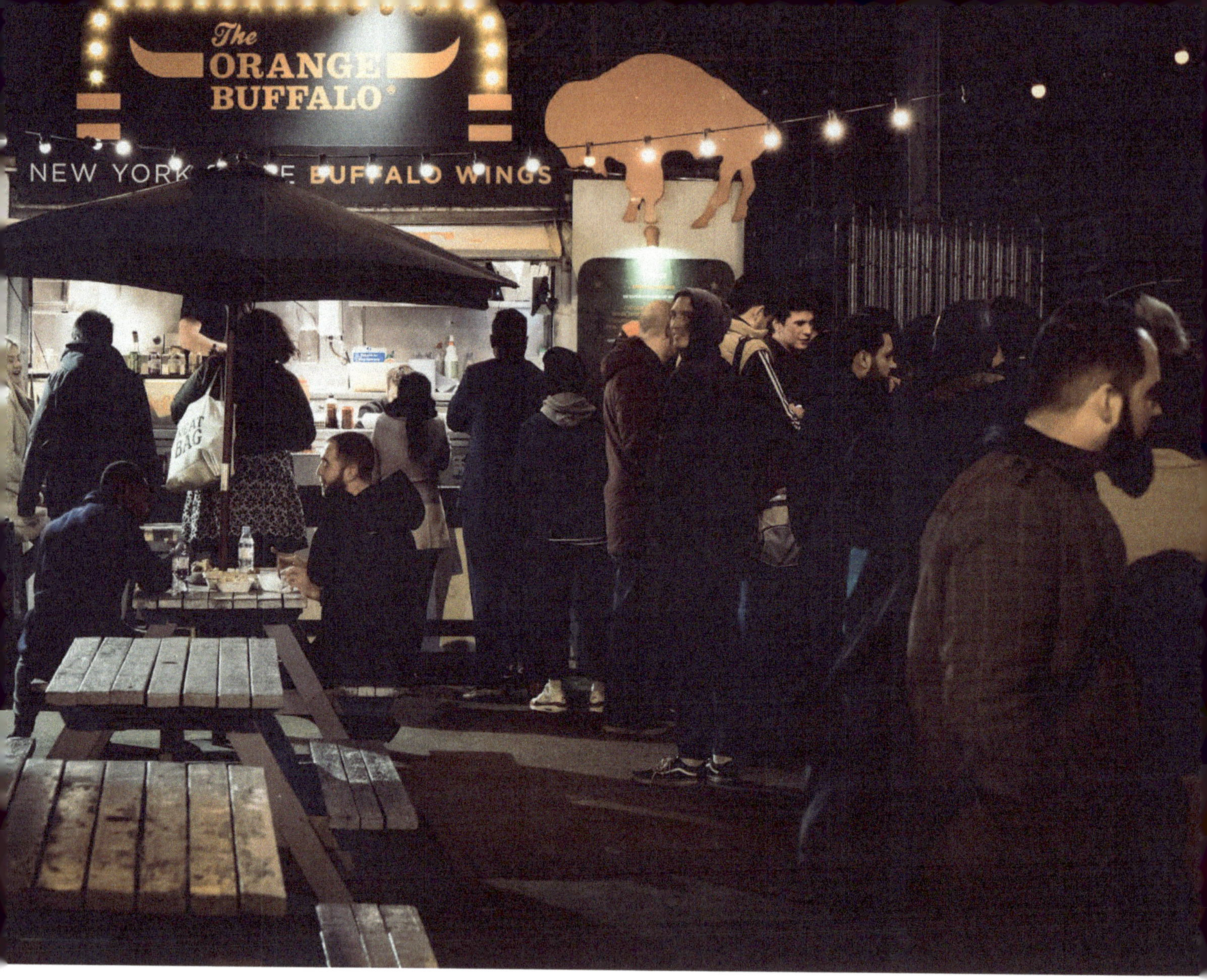

Shoreditch

Photo by Paul Hudson

Shoreditch is one of London's trendiest areas, located to the east of central London. Shoreditch's Brick Lane Market is home to food stands (pictured), vintage clothing shops and a huge number of curry houses. The area has gone through rapid gentrification in the 2010s and its architecture is quickly starting to mirror the nearby financial district.

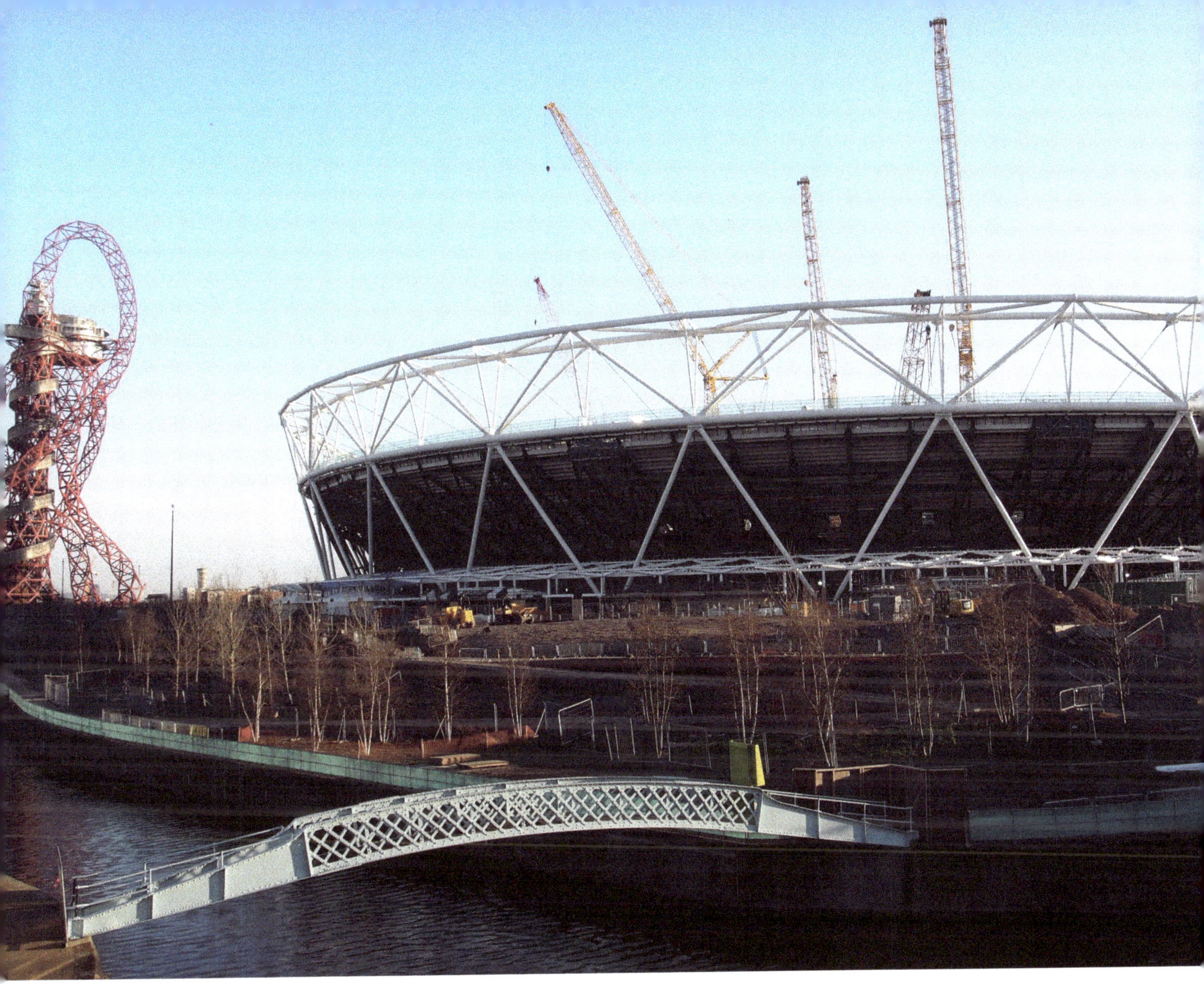

Queen Elizabeth Olympic Park

Photo by Velike Britanija

This 560-acre park was built for London's 2012 Olympic and Paralympic Games. As of 2018, the main stadium is now used by football team West Ham United, and holds other events such as concerts. To the left of the picture is the ArcelorMittal Orbit, Britain's largest piece of public art, which contains a viewing platform and the world's longest slide.

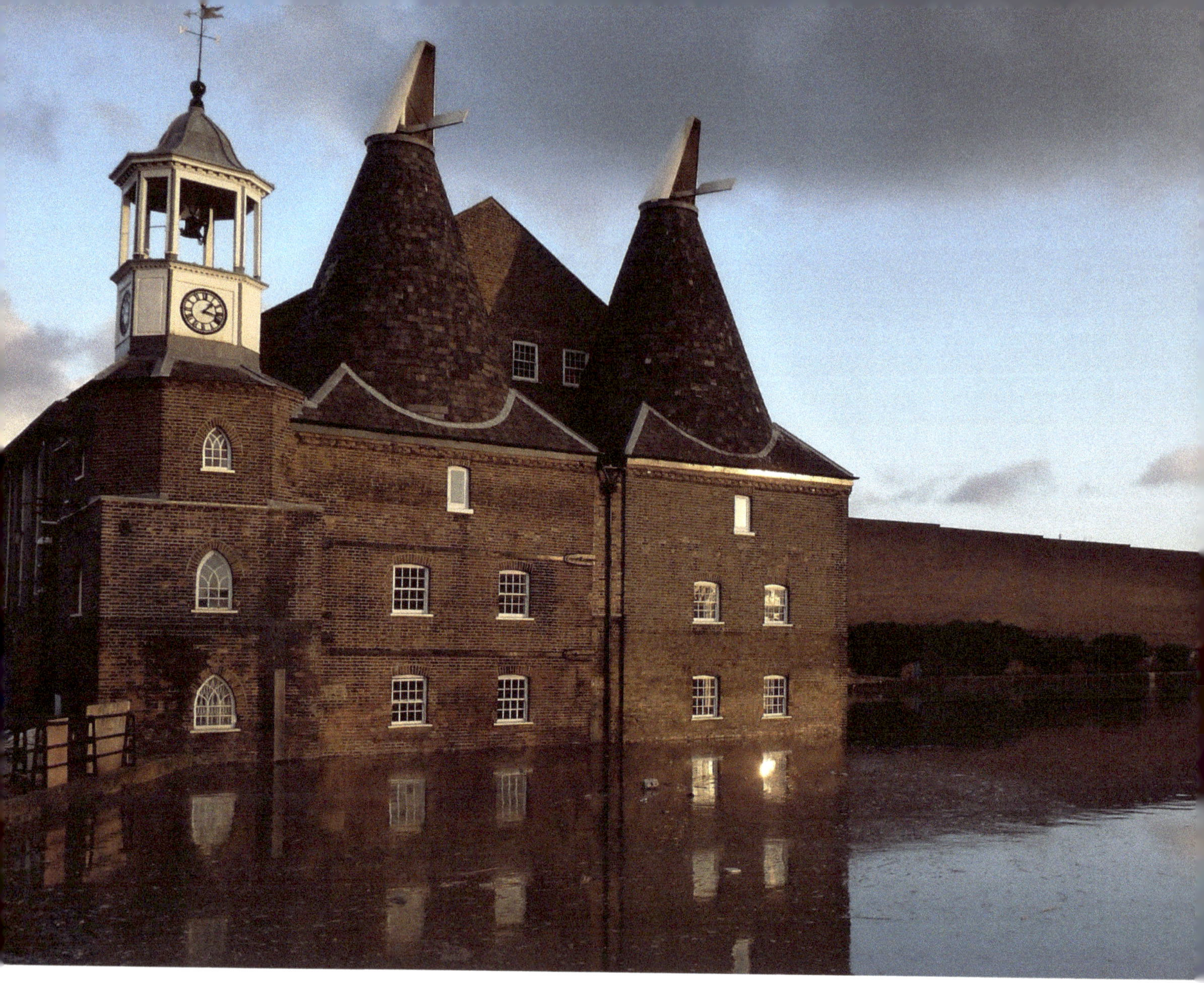

Three Mills

Photo by Gordon Joly

Pictured is the Clock Mill, part of an area called Three Mills on the River Lea, where in the past tidal mills were used to ground flour for the bakers in the local area. The Clock Mill is today used by East London Science School. The building dates from the 19th century, though the clock and bell are older. The House Mill stands nearby (not pictured).

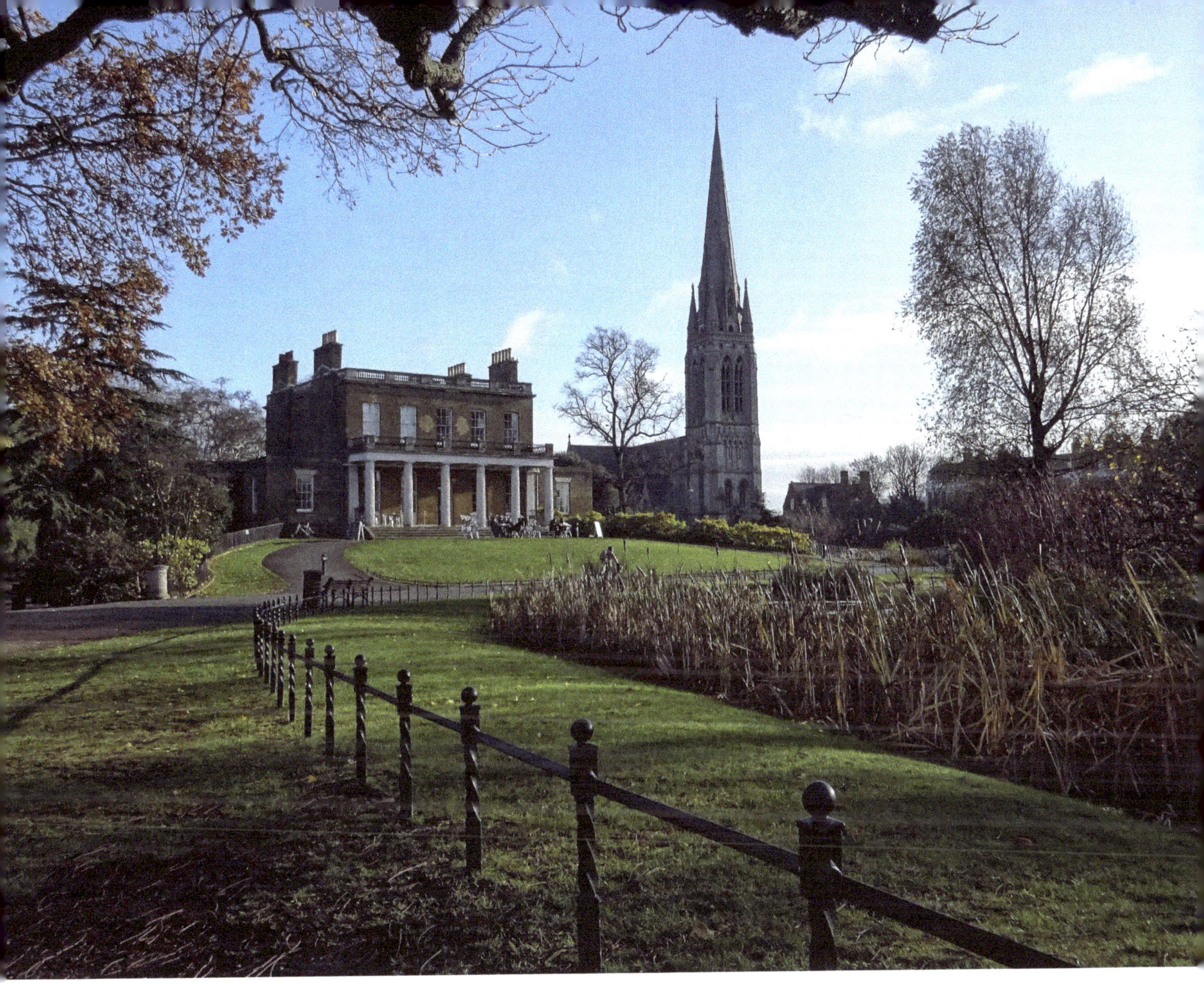

Photo by David Holt

Clissold Park

Clissold Park spans 55 acres and is located in Stoke Newington in north east London. Clissold House (pictured) dates from the 18th century and was built for Jonathan Hoare, a merchant. Today the building is used as a cafe and events venue. The spire of St Mary's New Church can also be seen, in the background, dating from the 19th century.

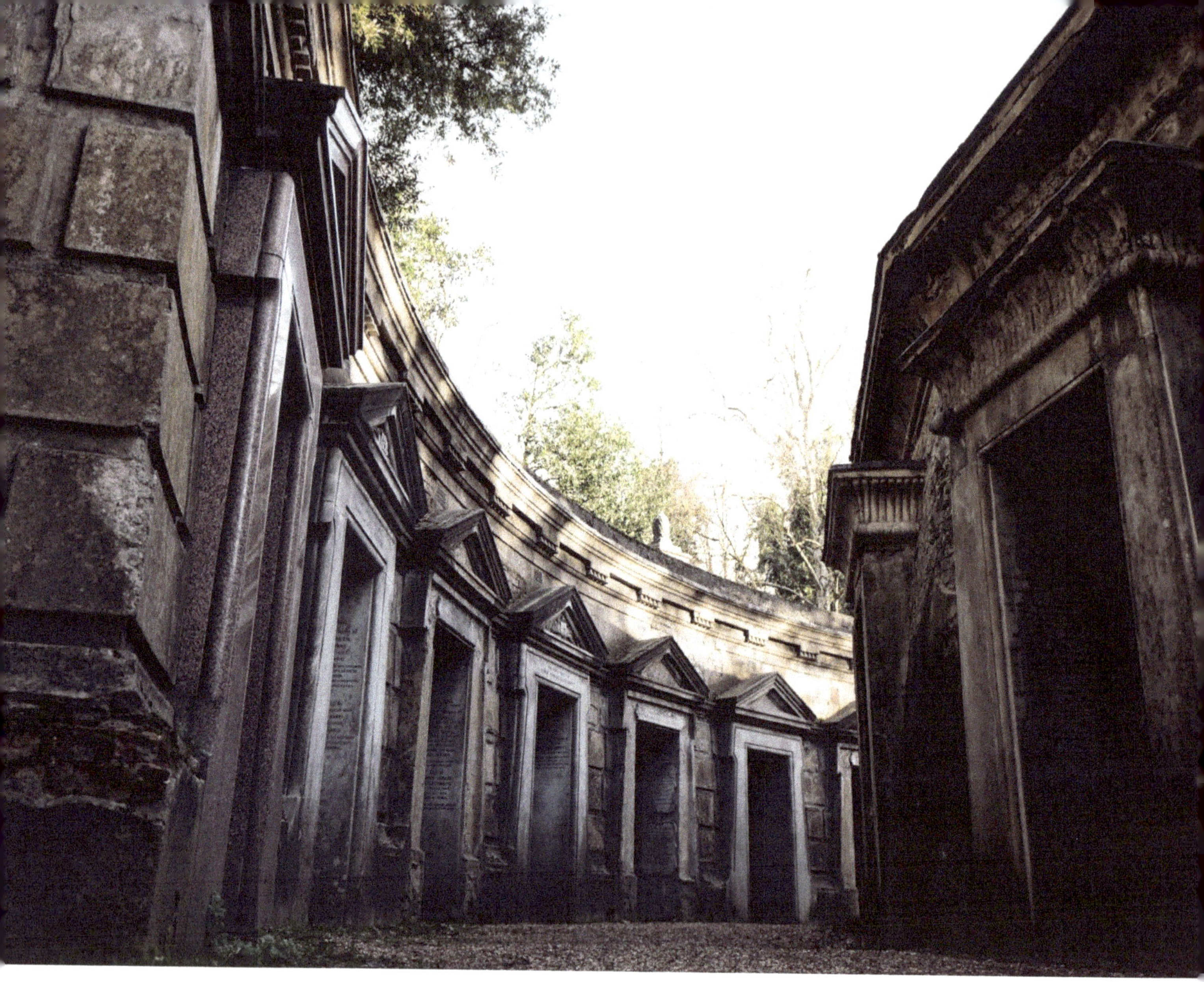

Highgate Cemetery

Photo by Elizabeth Ellis

Highgate Cemetery is one of London's most unusual sights - over 170,000 people are buried here in 53,000 graves. Pictured is the Circle of Lebanon area of the West Cemetery. You can also see the catacombs, Egyptian Avenue and the beautiful mausoleum of Julius Beer. Notably buried in the East Cemetery is Karl Marx. The cemetery dates from 1839.

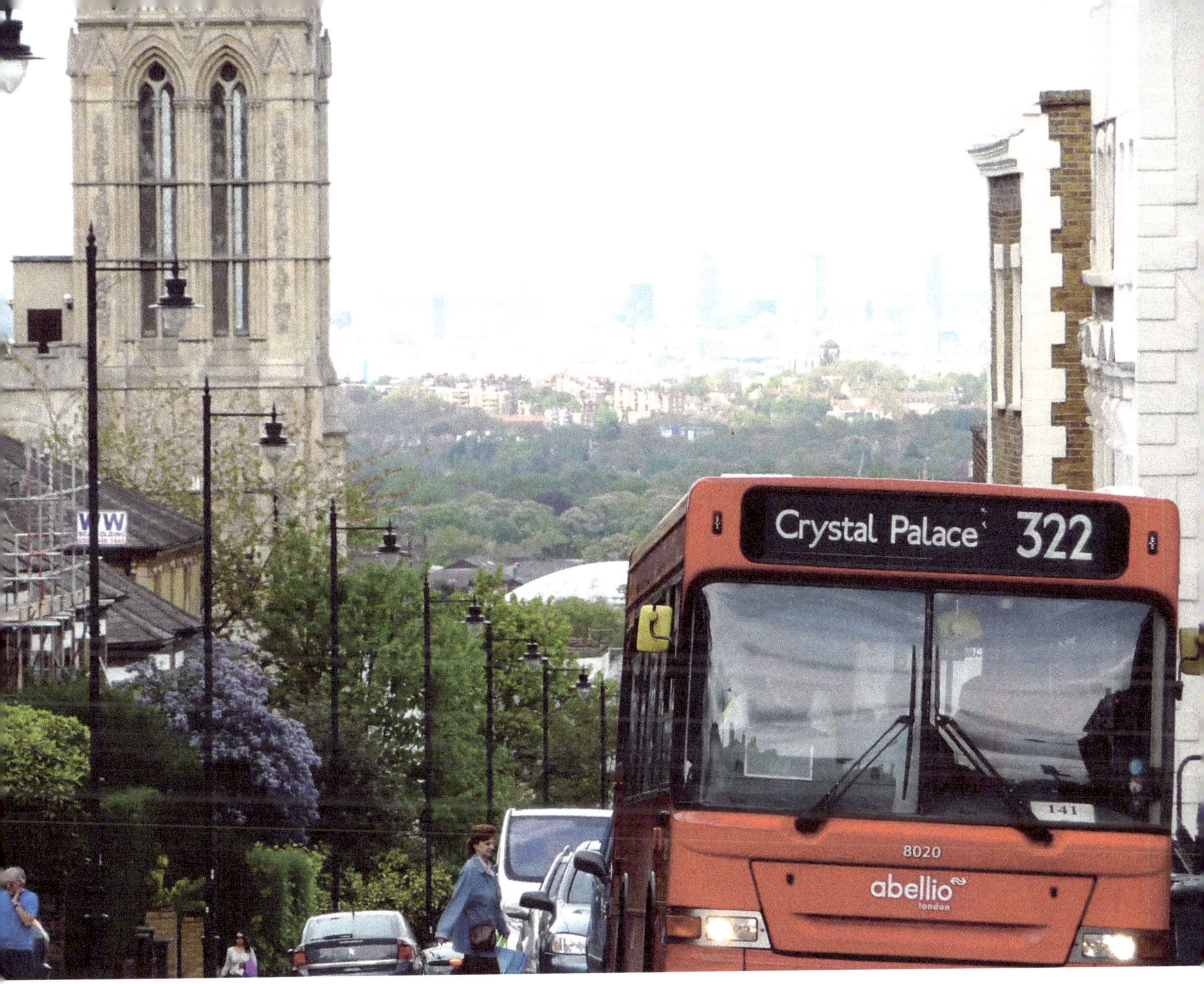

Photo by Cpt. Roger Fenton

Gipsy Hill

Gipsy Hill is located in south London and is named after the gypsies who frequented this area. The tower of Christ Church Gipsy Hill is pictured with a view of central London beyond, including notably St. Paul's Cathedral. The area borders Crystal Palace which was home to The Crystal Palace between 1854 and 1936 when it burned down in a fire.

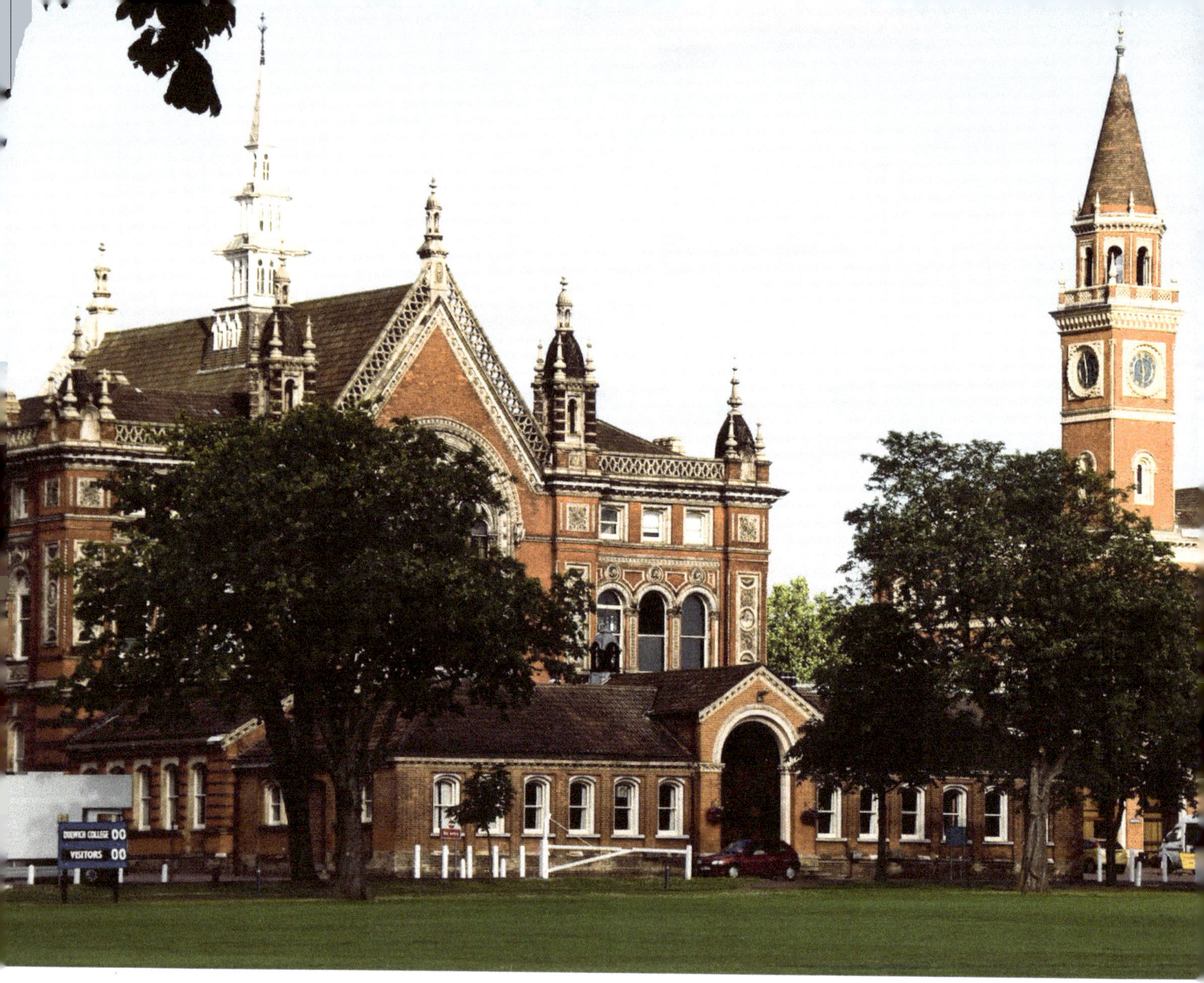

Dulwich

Photo by Herry Lawford

Dulwich is an area of south London which has been inhabited since at least the 10th century. Notable in the area is Dulwich College (pictured) which was founded in 1619, although the current buildings date from the 19th century. This all-boys school counts Nigel Farage (former UKIP leader) and author Sir P. G. Wodehouse amongst its alumni.

www.ingramcontent.com/pod-product-compliance
Ingram Content Group UK Ltd.
Pitfield, Milton Keynes, MK11 3LW, UK
UKHW061951290726
14090UKWH00021B/1171

9 781987 671155